World economic and social activities have grown rapidly in the first years of the "Development Decade," and international conferences, attended by the world's leading scientists, economists, and educators have been unanimous in reaching two basic conclusions: First, there exists a widening gap between the wealthy nations and the poor nations; secondly, this gap—of concern to all nations—can be bridged only by the most drastic measures of international co-operation.

The UN has already quietly assembled a body of new knowledge and an action program which are vital to man's future. The general public knows too little about the UN's central role in helping to build world prosperity through aid to under-developed nations. WORLD OF PROMISE is the story of these ideas and action. This is the first time so varied an account of current UN activity has been summarized for the general reader.

In nontechnical language, Dr. Joyce has outlined the development of economic, social, technical and educational programs. Technical Assistance in nearly 100 countries is emphasized, including its backing by the Special Fund in over 400 projects, and its support by the World Bank. The growing necessity for international co-operation under UN auspices is highlighted in contrast to the sometimes politically motivated policies of direct "foreign aid."

Here is an indispensable handbook — for newspaper readers, educators, and all engaged in public affairs. The many-sided program of world co-operation is shown in the perspective that has led to International Co-operation Year, inaugurated by the UN at the beginning of 1965.

WORLD OF PROMISE

A Guide to the United Nations Decade of Development

By

James Avery Joyce

Introduction by
David Owen
Executive Chairman
Technical Assistance Board
United Nations

1965
Oceana Publications, Inc.
Dobbs Ferry, New York

Prefatory Note

This little book is an introduction to a big subject, which becomes more complicated every day. For the U.N. is a fast-developing organization. Increasing demands are being made upon it from every quarter of the globe—not least from the developing countries, as they are called.

As its activities reach further and further afield, it is natural that a special terminology should grow up around its various functions and departments. All big organizations tend to develop a jargon of their own, which their officials use as a kind of official shorthand for their internal purposes.

But the aim of these pages is a limited one: it is to help the general reader and, particularly, the teacher or student, to gain a clear and simple picture of how the U.N. and its family of economic and social agencies are assisting the human race towards better living conditions across the planet.

The working machinery behind this endeavour necessarily involves a number of U.N. committees, sub-committees, and other active units, which—as befits a democratic organization—operate on the basis of resolutions, reports, and supporting documentation.

An occasional diagram may serve to clarify these groupings and relationships and obviate lengthy descriptions of organizational machinery in the main text.

As this book has been written before the merger of the Special Fund and the UN Technical Assistance programme has been completed, it has been thought best to deal with that topic briefly in the last chapter only.

The following chapters are confined, therefore, to the main working principles of the Development Decade and the general structure of the leading agencies—especially the World Bank, the Special Fund, and Technical Assistance—which have been closely associated in a common program. To this has been added a summary account of the mammouth U.N. Conference on Trade and Development which took place in Geneva in mid-1964, and some indication of the many operational problems which lie ahead.

The specialist will look for detailed information in the official records of the Organization or in the more advanced brochures and text-books, which are readily available for the serious student. The general reader who wants to take the subject further can select for his needs from the publications listed in the Booklist at the end.

—J.A.J.

Acknowledgements

This book is based mainly on material issued by various "branches" of the U.N. family, especially from the World Bank, the Special Fund, and the Technical Assistance Board. The booklist at the end includes some of the publications which have been instrumental in its preparation. Responsibility for the material selected from so rich a store and for the way in which it is presented rests, of course, entirely with the author. Nonetheless, the author is particularly indebted to advice given by and for consultations with the World Bank, and, at United Nations Headquarters, with the Special Fund, the Technical Assistance Board, the Department of Economic and Social Affairs, and the Office of Public Information. Above all the author expresses his gratitude for the constant encouragement received from the Chief of Special Projects, United Nations, with whom the book was originally planned and who conceived the necessity and purpose of the book in the first place, and who pursued its production in close co-operation with the UN Office of Public Information, the Public Liaison Division of UNESCO and Consultative Committee for Public Information of the United Nations.

This book also forms Volume VI of the Oceana-United Nations Study Guide Series, the material for which was assembled under the auspices of UNESCO in co-operation with the United Nations and the other UN organizations covered in the series.

(See complete list on page 164 of this volume)

All photographs have been reprinted by courtesy of the United Nations.

Permission to reprint brief extracts from the following publications is gratefully acknowledged from the publishers designated: *America and the World Revolution*, by A. J. Toynbee: Oxford University Press, New York, 1962; *The Attack on World Poverty*, Andrew Shonfield: Vintage Books, Random House, New York, 1962 *Challenge of Affluence*, by Gunnar Myrdal: Pantheon Books, New York, 1963; *Restless Nations*, A Symposium of the Council on World Tensions: Dodd, Mead and Company, New York, 1962; *The United Nations and How It Works*, by D. C. Coyle: New American Library of World Literature, Inc., New York, 1964; *World Without Want*, by Paul G. Hoffman: Harper and Row, Inc., New York, 1962.

•

The illustrations at the beginning of each chapter are some of the U.N. stamps issued by the United Nations Postal Administration, United Nations. N.Y.

By the same Author

The Story of International Co-operation

Challenge of the Decade of Development

Revolution on East River

Red Cross International

Now is the Time

Justice at Work

Capital Punishment: A World View

Youth Faces the New World

Education and Training (United Nations)

Labour Faces the New Age (I.L.O.)

Studies in U.N. Charter Revision (ed.)

World Organization—Federal or Functional (symposium)

Contents

Introduction to
"WORLD OF PROMISE"

This book appears at a particularly crucial period, when people need to be made aware, not only why the decade of the 1960's has been called the U.N. Development Decade, but what all nations hope to achieve by it. The dramatic significance of the constructive work of the U.N. Family of Agencies may be something of a surprise for most of the people who come face to face with it for the first time.

A dozen years ago, when the U.N. family was first beginning to mobilize assistance to the developing countries, pins were placed in a large wall map in a room on the 29th floor of the United Nations building in New York. They showed where each adviser or technician was assigned. The colour of the pin indicated whether he was an agronomist, an engineer, a meterologist, a malariologist or other specialist, and a smaller pin denoted the award of a fellowship to the national of a developing country.

Today, the map—a visual symbol of an intensely human undertaking—is almost obscured by a mass of multi-coloured pins which splash over southern Europe, across the Near and Far East, and down into Latin America and Africa.

Those of us who are preoccupied with the administrative and financial complexities of technical assistance have received a growing satisfaction from the story that map has told. The bands of colour have grown denser as Governments have requested more U.N. assistance, and become brighter as more international Agencies have entered the field. Requests which at the start came from 50 or so countries eventually came from 125 or more.

In the 1960's, the establishment of the United Nations Special Fund, under the direction of Paul G. Hoffman, doubled the concentration of activity, opening many avenues to pre-investment, as will be explained in this book. Similarly, the World Bank and its affiliates have provided more and more of the capital which is so badly needed by the nations of Asia, Africa and Latin America.

If this progress has been a source of gratification to those of us on the inside, how much more has it meant to the millions of individuals whom we are trying to serve?

The story of how these manifold endeavours began and their increasing impact on the developing world is contained in this book. Presented in the author's own style and on the basis of his personal observation, the narrative covers the main outlines of the U.N. family's part in the unfolding drama of our times. I believe that, as a basic guide, "World of Promise" will be of service both to the United Nations and to the individual reader.

DAVID OWEN
Executive Chairman
Technical Assistance Board
United Nations

The Great Paradox

"Speaking as a physician," said Dr. F. T. Sai of Ghana, at the United Nations Conference on Science and Technology for Development, held in Geneva in 1963, "I should like to ask what good it will do a mother to develop one half of a pair of Siamese twins and leave the other half? When the time of reckoning comes, she is sure to lose both." And the President of the same conference, Professor M.S. Thacker of India, extended the analogy by saying: "Just as we cannot accept the existence of a slum at the end of our garden, so we cannot, or should not, tolerate poverty next door to abundance."[1]

This "gap" between the rich nations and the poor nations has been the constant theme of every important gathering of scientists or economists or educators held anywhere in the world during the last dozen years or longer. Its existence is the Categorical Negative of our times. Because such a paradox challenges every thoughtful mind today, no-one confronted by it has failed to ask the inevitable question: *"What shall we do about it?"*

That is why this book has been written.

In fact, such gatherings of concerned specialists as the international scientific conference mentioned above, have done more than stimulate enquiry as to the probable causes of and possible cures for this phenomenon; they have begun to develop a conviction—implicit in both the quotations at the beginning of this chapter—that this small planet of ours can no longer get along with itself, half poor, half rich. It is the compelling interest of all

---

[1] *World of Opportunity* (Vol. I of *Science and Technology for Development* series) United Nations, New York, 1963.

1

peoples alike to get rid of the glaring discrepancies which have, whatever their origins, split the planet into two unequal halves.

The veteran historian, Arnold Toynbee, has declared: "We are now moving into a chapter of human history in which our choice is going to be, not between a whole world and a shredded-up one, but between one world and no world. I believe that the human race is going to choose life and good, not death and evil."[2]

This one-world-or-none philosophy has, indeed, gained steady acceptance since the Second World War. For one reason, the proliferation of weapons of mass-annihilation has revealed to more and more people the sheer lunacy of relying on *them* to preserve global peace. But the idea has been growing, too, that in the economic sphere prosperity also is one and indivisible. Such is the general thesis of the chapters that follow.

Professor Abdus Salam in his address to the 1963 Geneva Conference told how "nine hundred years ago the great physician of Islam, Al Asuli, writing in distant Bokhara, divided his pharmacopoeia into two parts: 'Diseases of the Rich' and 'Diseases of the Poor'. If Al Asuli were alive today and could write about the afflictions of mankind, I am sure he would again plan to divide his pharmacopoeia into the same two parts. Half his treatise would speak of the one affliction of Rich Humanity—the psychosis of nuclear annihilation. The other half would be concerned with the one affliction of the Poor—their hunger and near starvation. In diagnosis, he might perhaps add that the two afflictions spring from a common cause: the excess of science in one case and the lack of science in the other. I wish, in prognosis, he may not have to add that it is the faltering will of the scientist-physician which needs building up much more than that of the patient."[3]

AN ALL-ROUND PICTURE

The main purpose of the present book is to show by many concrete examples how the effort to narrow this gap between "the excess of science" and the lack of it is being advanced by those instruments of world co-operation which nowadays are referred to increasingly under the title of the "United Nations

[2] *New York Times Magazine*, 5 April 1964.
[3] *Natural Resources* (Vol. II of *Science and Technology for Development* series), United Nations, New York, 1963.

family." Obviously, in an elementary survey of the work of the international agencies which are jointly seeking a down-to-earth answer to the foregoing question, only the key points of the United Nations development programme can be touched upon. For their activities are legion and as various as human need is unpredictable and insistent.

The separate branches of the family—Specialized Agencies, Special Fund, Technical Assistance Board, and others dealt with in this book—have all thrown up a fascinating literature of their own. But much of this is congealed in the cold terminology of their official records. However, the diligent student may usually have access to the reports, books, and brochures, which are happily symptomatic of the widening public interest in the United Nations affairs today. Yet sometimes it is useful for the general reader to be accorded a bird's-eye view of the development process, as seen from the vantage point of the United Nations. That is why, in the following pages, a broad survey is attempted of the machinery of the United Nations development programme as a whole, as it appears to be shaping through the late 1960's, and especially as it operates out in the field for the benefit of untold millions of "We, the Peoples".

From this general picture of the "Development Decade"—to give its official title—at least four major propositions can be seen to emerge, all of which will have a place in these chapters:

First, economic and social development today is a global problem and, as such, has to be organized on a world basis;

Second, basic resources are unevenly exploited and unfairly distributed across the earth, and this imbalance cannot be tolerated;

Third, competitive warfare budgets, which are burdening the big industrialized nations, are among the main obstacles to economic advance and so the aim should be to switch to welfare co-operation instead;

Fourth, education, in its fullest sense, is indispensable if the nations' leaders are to achieve the world-wide objectives of the Development Decade and if their peoples are to develop the skills and understanding needed to realize their particular national goals.

Fundamental to everything else is the discovery that, given peace, universal prosperity *is an attainable goal.*

Because of the primacy of this postulate, this chapter has begun with several citations from the United Nations Conference on Science and Technology for Development, held in Geneva in the Spring of 1963, which brought 2,000 scientists, economists and educators together. One of the conclusions which resulted from that epoch-making enquiry into Man's Family Estate (as one scientist termed it) was that man could master his material world —if he had the will to do so. The discussions in every section of the Conference, especially as to the elementary facts relating to the earth's resources, brought out this awareness of having to share together and to husband as one human family the living space and materials of a minor planet "round which a piece of man-conceived ironmongery can travel sixteen times a day".

"In the past, civilizations developed in localities or regions; they flourished and declined, but always another civilization could succeed them somewhere else. The Conference was, in terms of jobs of work to be done, a recognition that there is now a global civilization. It is not bounded by the Tigris and the Euphrates; it is the whole world, it is a closed community now so interdependent that every mistake made can be exaggerated on a world-wide scale and every opportunity seized, in corporate wisdom, can mutually bnefit the world of mankind."[4]

The promise of this world-scale development came out again and again as the scientists opened the secret treasures of their respective disciplines. It was pointed out, for instance, by Dr. Albert Parker of the United Kingdom, that "a study of the available data shows that for the world as a whole there are ample resources of commercial forms of energy. The total of the measured, indicated and inferred reserves of coal and lignites, even assuming that only a third can be economically recovered, is about 1,200 times the present annual consumption. Similar reserves of petroleum are equal to at least 60 times the present annual consumption. In addition, there are large reserves of oil

[4] *World of Opportunity* (Vol. I of *Science and Technology for Development* series), United Nations, New York, 1963.

4

in the oil shales and bituminous sands that have hardly been touched, because the extraction of the oil has not been economic while ample supplies of petroleum have been available. The measured and indicated reserves of natural gas are equal to more than a hundred and fifty times the present annual consumption."[5]

Apart from the fossil fuels which can be mined, and the hydro-electricity which can be won from flowing surface water, the scientists at Geneva were mindful too that tomorrow's power resources will include the sun and the winds. Although the sun represents the main source of energy which makes all life possible on this planet, its use for production of power is still not industrially significant. Because the sun's rays are diffused, they have to be reconcentrated as heat. And the Geneva story proceeds:

An Indian demonstrator finds that the boiling time of water is ten minutes in a pressure cooker over a solar cooker at the National Physical Laboratory in New Delhi. Diesel fuel in an Indian village costs approximately $80 a ton, but solar power, at 15 cents a kilowatt hour, is a cheaper source of energy.

[5] *Op. cit.*

"Archimedes set fire to the Roman fleet, besieging Syracuse, by focussing the sun's rays with burning glasses. The Incas used concave mirrors to light dry tinder for their fire-and-smoke signals which could transmit messages over a distance of more than 2,000 miles in less than three hours. Today, giant mirrors can be used to smelt ores and produce points of heat of an intensity which can bore a hole in armour plating. To collect and concentrate the diffused rays, the mirrors have to be immense. Promising ventures have, economically, captured enough of the heat rays to produce low-pressure steam for limited industrial purposes. In areas of sustained and intense sunlight, solar energy has been used to heat water and to cool houses and provide refrigeration—ice from the sun!"[6]

NEW ENERGY — NEW PERSPECTIVES

Ever since the first United Nations Conference on the Peaceful Uses of Atomic Energy, held in Geneva in 1955, nations which are conscious of the need of more power for their expanding economy and their increasing populations have looked to the development of nuclear power with rising hopes. Recent advances in nuclear physics and experience of the operation of power plants that use uranium as fuel have strengthened these hopes. In fact, large nuclear reactors (i.e. atomic furnaces) have already been in operation for some years in the advanced countries and dozens of smaller research reactors are in operation in other lands. Thousands of scientists and skilled operators are being trained to operate them, and the costs—which are the present major obstacle—have been steadily reduced and are now almost competitive with coal in some cases, even where coal is plentiful and cheap.[7]

The International Atomic Energy Agency (IAEA) of Vienna presented to the 1963 Geneva Conference the prospect which follows:

"A further increase in nuclear power capacity is at present in preparation in all areas of the world, developed and less developed. The planning of nuclear power stations is already at an advanced stage in some of the developing countries,

---

[6] op. cit·
[7] See Proceedings of the International Conference on the Peaceful Uses of Atomic Energy (16 volumes), United Nations, New York, 1956.

6

including Brazil, India, Pakistan and the Philippines. For 1966 it is expected that the total capacity of nuclear power in the world will be 9.5 million kw, increasing to 15 million to 18 million kw in 1970.

"The main reason for the interest in nuclear energy is that it has been technically proven as a new source of electric power. The consumption of electric power has in most under-developed countries increased very sharply and more rapidly than the total consumption of energy. The possible market for nuclear power in these areas is therefore growing significantly."

During the 1970's and 1980's, nuclear energy should become the cheapest source of power over a steadily widening field, Sir William Penney (leader of the United Kingdom delegation) declared at the Third International Conference on the Peaceful Uses of Atomic Energy, which brought to Geneva experts from over 80 countries in September, 1964. The Conference revealed that nuclear power was already competitive with conventional power in several regions, and that, from about 1970 onward, industrial nations and some developing countries will rely on it increasingly for much of their power requirements.

THE ACCELERATION OF HISTORY

Beyond these expanding hopes in the field of technology, one is brought face to face with what might be called the acceleration of history. It should be borne in mind that scientific research, which played only a marginal role in the Nineteenth Century, has become so important in the Twentieth Century that it is no longer possible to describe any modern economic development without according it its rightful place. A UNESCO expert has remarked: "The actual increase in the rapidity with which discoveries follow one upon another may be regarded as one facet of the acceleration of history, an acceleration which has been evident throughout the evolution of human societies. It is clear, however, that scientific activity, with all its technical and economic consequences, is at present passing through a period of particularly rapid development as compared with other human activities and may, broadly speaking, be said to be doubling in the course of each decade.[8]

[8] Pierre Auger: *Current Trends in Scientific Research*, UNESCO, Paris, 1961.

7

The above quotations refer only to some of the energy "potentials" of our planet, and may therefore seem to present a one-sided picture. But such data—which was not available a decade ago and which still today has not broken through the time-lags which pervade the mystic realm of foreign policy—calls for an entirely fresh look at the basic problems of world economic development.

In the perspective of history it may well be seen that the temporary "advance" which created our Western prosperity and produced the present disparity between us and the rest of mankind is the result of a socio-scientific process which dates from the steam engine—itself contemporary with political revolutions, including the emergence of the United States from colonial status in 1776. Hence, the industrial development of Britain barely 200 years ago; that of Western Europe 150 years ago; that of the United States 100 years ago; that of Japan 80 years ago; that of Russia, with the Soviet Revolution, 40 years ago. Forty years from now we shall have entered the Twenty-First Century. How different will be the picture of world disparity when the "underdeveloped" countries (as many people designate them today) enter the Twenty-First Century!

NEWLY-AROUSED CONTINENTS

To these materialistic considerations must be added the spiritual awakening of the "new" countries, which is bound to prove as soul-shaking to the "old" countries too—and certainly to the Western world, which is largely obsessed with maintaining its *status quo.* An American economist has drawn attention to the implications of this revolution of economic development, as he terms it:

> "Of all the changes which have taken place in the Twentieth Century, none is so charged with long-term significance as the revolution of economic development. Within the span of a single generation, two-thirds of the world has acquired political and economic self-consciousness, a phenomenon without parallel in human affairs. And this extraordinary awakening portends more than a mere widening of our historic field. Implicit as well, in the emergence of self-consciousness on a global scale, is a shift in the locus of the history-making process itself. The outbreak of the revolution of

economic development signals a slow movement of the dynamic core of world events away from the Northern and Western nations into the broad new areas of the South and East. Regardless of the outcome of the cold war—and certainly in the advent of a hot war—the main current of historic evolution will henceforth increasingly reflect the emerging societies of the newly-aroused continents."[9]

The key phrase in the above quotation is probably "the emergence of self-consciousness on a global scale". For the most alarming feature of under-development is the fact that the gap between the developed and the less-developed countries is, generally speaking, *increasing* in terms of real income per head. And this is happening at a time when "mass-communication" means just that: communication to the masses.

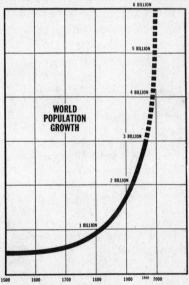

WORLD POPULATION GROWTH

One method of measuring the gap is by comparing average incomes. In North America personal incomes *average* $2,500 a year, while in Europe they amount to about $900 a year. In most Asian and African countries the figure is between $50 and $100 a year. A comparison of total incomes set against population (see *Statistics of Hunger*, Food and Agriculture Organization, 1952)

[9] *The American Scholar*, Autumn 1962, "The Revolution of Economic Development" by Robert L. Heilbroner.

9

gives a simple picture of how current wealth is distributed around the world:

Region	Per cent of world income	Per cent of world population
North America	39.8	6.7
Europe	37.7	22.2
Far East	12.3	52.3
Latin America	4.7	6.8
Africa	2.2	7.1

Over the last half century there has been, in fact, little change in real income per head in most of Asia—the home of over half the world's population. Real income has risen considerably in the United States, Western Europe, and a few high-income countries elsewhere, such as Canada, Australia, and the white portion of South Africa. The picture with regard to these extremes in incomes is clear enough; but when appraising these contrasts we should not forget that even an equal rate of growth would widen the absolute gap. Dr. Jan Tinbergen, Director of the Netherlands Economic Institute, appropriately states:

"To understand what these figures mean in simple human terms, we must realize that most of the people in Asia and Africa and many in Latin America are living at starvation level. Their consumption is some 10 per cent of that in developed countries and they are in a constant fight against hunger and illness. Everything in their budget—food, clothing, housing, education, amusement—is far below adequate standards as we see them. For a long time these people have been forced by circumstances and encouraged by philosophies, partly geared to their situation, to accept their condition as natural. Increasing contact with the wealthier parts of the world is now raising a question in their minds as to the necessity for their underprivileged status, and it seems clear that once this doubt has worked its way through the population we shall witness justified attempts to change the situation—attempts which may be carried out with an energy corresponding to the tensions endured. It is because such basic human issues are involved for such a large number of people that this problem is so important. It deserves to be our main preoccupation."[10]

[10] Jan Tinbergen: *Shaping the World Economy*, 20th Century Fund, New York, 1962.

A HUNGRY WORLD

Ideas are furiously on the march; and there is nothing (insisted Victor Hugo) more powerful than an idea whose day has arrived. Set against the world of promise, for millions to see, stands the world of penury in stark and ugly contrast.

Today, more than three billion people live on earth. About one and one-half *billion* of all these people are ill-fed. Mostly, these ill-fed people are getting too little food for a happy, healthy life; many are continually hungry and some are starving. Others may be getting enough food, but not the right kinds. Their diets lack body-building foods, like eggs and meat and milk, and certain protective vitamins. They don't feel hungry, but they suffer from various deficiency diseases which weaken them, reduce their productivity and shorten their lives. These ill-fed people of the world live mostly in Asia, in the Middle East, in Africa, and in Latin America.

Now the pressure of growing population poses a new problem to complicate these age-old food shortages. Throughout man's history the population of the earth has grown slowly. In this century, however, medical advances have resulted in more people living longer and the population of the world has started to grow much faster than it has ever grown before. It took about one hundred years for the population of the world to double between 1800 and 1900. It took only sixty years for it to double again between 1900 and 1960. It will take only about 35 years to double again. At the end of this century there will be not three billion, but more than six billion people living on the face of the earth.°

The hunger challenge presents, therefore, a double problem. There are already one-and-a-half billion people in the world who are ill fed and something must immediately be done to improve their diets. But, in addition, about three billion extra people will be in the world in less than 40 years. So we must plan *how* to feed them too.

But can this be done?

THE VICIOUS CIRCLE

Before an answer is attempted to this basic question, it may be useful to pursue further, in the remainder of this chapter, the great paradox which stands like a mocking spectre before the anxious eyes of the ordinary human being living in the underdeveloped regions. He has a life expectancy of 40 years at best—in some countries only 27—against 63 in the advanced countries. He has an income of less than one-tenth of that enjoyed in the developed regions. He must subsist on an average daily diet of only 700 calories above sheer starvation level—at least 750 calories below that of the fortunate upper third of mankind.

He is caught in a vicious circle. He lacks bread, yet his primitive agriculture yields him only six bushels of wheat per acre—

° World population was estimated at 3,135 million in mid-1962, compared with 2,509 million in 1950, and 2,893 million in 1958. Asia (excluding the USSR) contains 56.3 per cent of the world total and Oceania has the smallest population (less than 1 per cent). Europe and North and South America accounted for 27.5 per cent. Over the period 1958-1962, world population has increased at the annual rate of 2 per cent. (From *U.N. Statistical Yearbook*, 1964.)

contrasted with 40 bushels in the "rich" countries. 50 per cent of his fellows are constantly ill; he himself is plagued by ill-health; yet there is only one doctor for each 20,000 persons—while the advanced countries, with developed medical services, have one physician for a thousand persons. And he cannot read. His children have no schools to go to. They are among at least four hundred millions of children of school age in the world today without classrooms or teachers or books.

He cannot break this vicious circle without outside help of a substantial and systematic kind. As Edmund Burke declared: "For big ills, small remedies are no remedy at all." That is the crux of the matter. That is where the world of promise comes to meet his situation through the new institutions of earth-wide cooperation which have so recently joined their forces within the Development Decade.

The gap cannot fill itself. The advance of modern science and technology, by itself, is *not* providing a bridge across it, as many people once imagined. There is nothing inevitable about "progress", if men do not produce it, guide it, share it.

In his opening address, the President of the 1963 Geneva Conference on Science and Technology for Development uttered this warning: "The wide, and in some cases tragic, gap can easily be gauged when one realizes that one-tenth of the peoples of the world enjoy 60 per cent of the world's income, while 57 per cent of them have less than 10 per cent of that wealth at their disposal. If present trends continue, the gulf between the poor and the rich countries of the world will widen still further; and this at a time when great continents have awoken to freedom and their populations are clamouring for certain minimum standards of life."

Dr. F. T. Sai, of Ghana, who was also quoted earlier, described this scandalous contrast in these terms: "We have seen that the two ends of the world's spectra of wealth and health are very far apart. We have used the term 'developed' and 'less-developed' to apply to these two ends . . . There are nations with a *per caput* income of $50 or less whilst others enjoy $1,000 or more."

THE SECRET KEY

The missing link between the two worlds, between modern

13

science and the needy areas, amounts to just this: How can the skills and the equipment, the money and the machines of the industrialized countries be *shared* with the non-industrialized economies?

There can be no doubt that the application of the expertise and the "know-how" of the advanced countries *can* transfrom the impoverished regions of the earth. Turning to the basic problem of agricultural development, we may ask what is the secret key which can unlock the poor nation's larder?

The answer can be seen, for example, in the situation of the few hundred million people who live mostly in the United States and Canada, in the countries of Western Europe and in Australia and New Zealand, who all enjoy ample quantities of a wide range of foods. It is not that they have *more land;* but much more food comes out of the American farm acre than out of the

Farmer sowing rice in a Ceylon field.

African farm acre. Nor are there *more people* working to produce the food. A Canadian farmer can provide a generous diet for about a dozen people; but an Asian farmer can barely do more than provide a meagre diet for his own family.

The specific answer is plainly in the application of science and technology to the production of food. Scientific agriculture produces more and better food from less land with less labour every year. This involves such things as the use of high quality seeds and cattle, which yield more food, and the use of fertilizers and irrigation. To make best use of these, highly educated farmers and farm machinery are needed. Farmlands must also be protected, so that they will not only produce ample food this year, but will be fertile and productive next year. There is no mystery here.

Yet this scientific agriculture has hardly touched the ill-fed countries of the world. They have, of course, realized the need for development in all fields of economic activity. But only within a brief span of years have they—in most cases—enjoyed even the political independence to begin nation building in earnest. Their agriculture is primitive and often has not changed in centuries. The awakening touch must come from outside; and it must come generously, efficiently, and purposefully.

How vast is the promise before these truly developing countries, when the industrialized nations beat their swords into ploughshares and their spears into pruning hooks for the world conquest of hunger, has been graphically put by Paul G. Hoffman:

> "There are dozens of rivers flowing through the low-income countries whose waters have never been used for irrigation or the generation of power. There are hundreds of millions of acres of land which could be made productive by the application of fertilizer. And there are other hundreds of millions of acres in semi-arid countries which could be made productive, if ways were found to conserve river water that now flows into the sea unused, or to take the salt out of the sea water inexpensively."[11]

---

[11] Paul G. Hoffman: *World Without Want*, Harper and Row, New York, 1962.

TWO MYTHS DEMOLISHED

Before we pass, in the next chapter, to consider the ways and means by which the United Nations family is waging this war against want on so many fronts, two related myths which sometimes dominate political thinking today in approaching the problems of development might at this point be demolished. The first is: "Can we *afford* it?"—meaning, are the industrialized nations able to finance it? And the second is: "Is the effort *worth it*?"— meaning, are we morally justified in attempting it?

It is true that many of the undertakings being promoted by the United Nations family will be measured, in subsequent chapters, in terms of dollars or other currencies. Yet it would be a mistake to think of these costs as actual outpourings of hard cash, which are extracted from the taxpayers of the wealthier countries and "lost" to those contributing. For one thing, a study of the contributions donated from the 108 countries making up the Special Fund pledges (see Chapter 6) would dispose of the fallacy that only a handful of rich countries carry the burden.

The need of the underdeveloped countries is for specific goods and services. Although these commodities and skills must obviously be paid for by the people of the donor country, such payments are, in effect, a subsidy to boost that country's own exports. It has always been this way. What we give, we receive back, sooner or later. Machines and equipment sent to the underdeveloped countries provide jobs for workers in the manufacturing nations. They also bring profits to industry through increased foreign trade. Similarly, experts who go abroad to assist another nation to build its markets and its trade, are earning their livelihood in the same sense as if they worked at home; their families and future careers will benefit from their overseas activity—and the world will be richer too.

The other myth assumes that advanced peoples can only help their weaker neighbours by some form of altruistic charity. It expresses a certain type of "lady bountiful" psychology, which seeks the obsequious gratitude due from an inferior to a superior. The truth is that the Development Decade represents a far vaster challenge to the human spirit than can be envisaged within the folkways of orthodox foreign policy. It offers a new philosophy of

16

world relationships which cannot but enoble all who are privileged to have however small a part in it.

It is to the implications of this wider challenge that the following chapters of this book are addressed. It has been epitomised by Barbara Ward in her essay on "New Perspectives", as follows:

"No great undertaking can be sustained without great ideas to inspire it. Our moral vision of mankind as a human family has to grow fast enough to catch up with the physical fact of a world united by science and technology and dwarfed by the opening vistas of outer space. If morals have any meaning at all they must entail that the hungry are fed, the naked clothed, the homeless sheltered, and all the sons of men given some little share in the world's great patrimony of knowledge and opportunity, of health and hope."[12]

---

[12] Quoted from the symposium, *Restless Nations*, Dodd, Mead & Co., New York, 1962.

2

Bridging The Gap –
The Development Decade

"Students of the development problems of underdeveloped countries are gradually finding out that those problems are much more serious than was believed", contends Professor Gunnar Myrdal, Director of the Institute for International Economic Studies in Stockholm: "Overshadowing everything else is the fact that in addition to, and as a basis for, a much increased capital flow to underdeveloped countries, what is really needed is a radical change on the part of the rich countries in their way of doing business with the underdeveloped countries".[1]

This call for a bold new approach to the development process has been widely echoed by concerned scientists and economists and educationalists in the Western world. They reject the notion, which is still accepted by the ordinary run of politician, that foreign aid is essentially a system of generous "hands-outs" to indigent peoples. Speaking at the International Conference on Tensions in Development, held at Oxford University in 1961, the remarks of Professor Max F. Millikan, of M. I. T., Boston, may be taken as indicative of that "creative innovation" in Western attitudes for which he was pleading:

> "In the past we have conceived of the problem of assisting development much too narrowly as the simple transfer from the developed to the underdeveloped countries of knowledge, technology, institutions, and practices in common use in the United States and Europe. Slowly and painfully, out of the

---

[1] Gunnar Myrdal: *Challenge to Affluence*, Pantheon Books, New York, 1963.

experience of ten years, we are coming to learn—in agriculture, in health, in industry, in political organization—that while the underdeveloped world has an enormous advantage in being able to draw upon the experience of the developed world accumulated since the Rennaissance, an adaption of that experience to the problems of the underdeveloped countries requires a process as creative, innovative, and experimental as any we went through."

It should always be remembered, of course, that international cooperation is coterminous with the history of mankind itself. The current operations of the United Nations family have, therefore, to be seen against the whole fabric of man's social evolution. They are not something apart. What we are witnessing today is not an emergency operation—limited in time, like a neat and compact Marshall Aid plan—but a rapid and spontaneous growth of institutions in the economic and social life of mankind which are an essential functional development of the United Nations political organization.

What these international agencies are attempting is an application to the world as a whole of those principles and practices of economic and technical development which have grown along with the other manifold institutions of Western civilization, while adapting them to the conditions of the "new" countries. As Arnold J. Toynbee has again pointed out: "Mankind's present-day experiment in Western Civilization may, in truth, be unique in some respects. For instance, this experiment is being conducted on a literally world-wide scale, and, as far as we know, this is the first time that this has happened."[2]

THE CONDITIONS OF PROGRESS

The great adventure of world service which is the subject of these pages was firmly laid down in the United Nations charter itself. Article 55 reads: "With a view to the creation of conditions of stability and well-being which are necessary for peaceful and friendly relations among nations, based on respect for the principle of equal rights and self-determination of the people, the United Nations shall promote . . . higher standards of living, full employment, and conditions of economic and social progress

[2] Arnold J. Toynbee: *America and the World Revolution*, Oxford U. P., New York and London, 1962.

and development". The next following Article pledges all members of the United Nations to take action to achieve these purposes.

On this solid foundation have been erected the day-to-day functions of the whole "UN family", as it has come to be called; and the main purpose of this chapter is to outline the formal structure of those "creative innovations", which have emerged so recently in response to˙ the hungry world portrayed in the first chapter.

Experience since the Second World War has abundantly shown that no single nation or group of nations, however "advanced", could deal effectively with the multiplicity of tasks involved in putting the underdeveloped world on its feet. Nor can any single world-wide institution, however well endowed with resources, tackle more than a small part of them. International cooperation has to be horizontal, as well as vertical, to bridge the gap—indeed, it has often to operate as if it were *supranational*.

There can be little doubt that what was an experimental and improvised effort launched by the United Nations and its agencies barely a decade ago, has already displayed the makings of a systematic long-term programme, whose ultimate goal is the economic and social enfranchisement of all peoples through world cooperation, in the broadest possible sense.[3]

MEMBERS OF THE FAMILY

It has been the practice of inter-governmental organizations to provide expert aid—generally in the form of visiting specialists—on the request of their Member States. The International Labour Organization, for example, began to provide experts in the field of labour legislation to Member States more than 30 years ago. The United Nations itself started its technical assistance activities as early as 1947, when nine countries were given help and advice in the form of social welfare services.

Direct aid under the United Nations began with the despatch of individual experts or teams of experts to meet requests coming from individual countries. This elementary system has since then evolved into an intricate but coordinated programme, in

---

[3] See further on this in the present author's *The Story of International Cooperation*, Franklin Watts, New York, 1964.

20

which many of the activities of the United Nations and its agencies are now integrated. It is not generally recognized, however, that much of the work of the United Nations is carried out in the "field", where over 80 per cent of its personnel is already working. Not unnaturally, with an increasing number of projects being carried out in cooperation with and between the Specialized Agencies, a continuous effort is required to coordinate the activities of the various types of organizations involved. This caution is needed not only to avoid duplication and to keep down costs, but, more significantly, to bring to bear on each local problem the specialized knowledge of the appropriate organizations.

We can now briefly review the special tasks of some of those agencies, which are most frequently referred to in this book.[4]

Practically all of the activities of the World Health Organization (WHO) can be characterized as technical assistance, in the sense that its efforts are focused on the eradiction of diseases, such as malaria, yaws, and leprosy. WHO aids the building up of national health services and the training of medical and technical personnel, as well as demonstrating new techniques for attacking and controlling diseases.

The United Nations Educational, Scientific and Cultural Organization (UNESCO) spends over $10 million annually on child and adult education and teacher training, as well as on the training of statisticians, educators and social scientists. It sponsors programmes of research directed at such problems as technical studies of arid land problems, and has set up regional scientific centres in Latin America, the Middle East, East and South-East Asia, to help raise the level of scientific knowledge in those areas.

Much of the technical assistance of the Food and Agriculture Organization (FAO) is carried out within the framework provided by regional and area offices located in Accra, Bangkok, Cairo, Mexico City, New Delhi, Rio de Janeiro, Santiago, and Washington. FAO's major activities include regional training centres and seminars covering such subjects as land reform, school-feeding, marketing of fisheries and farm produce, livestock improvement, and the use of radio-isotopes in agriculture. FAO also concentrates on controlling animal and plant diseases and pests.

---

[4] A complete list of their titles is included in *Appendix 3*.

Its present "Freedom-from-Hunger" campaign is an intensification of FAO's normal programme for increasing food production and improving nutrition. Under the World Food Programme, approximately $100 million in food, services, and cash are to be distributed through United Nations channels over a three-year period to underdeveloped areas to meet emergency situations and assist their programmes of economic development.

SOWING PEARLS

So much for a formal listing of some of the most useful members of the UN family. If all the different tasks undertaken by United Nations and Agency personnel in the developing countries during the past decade were put down on a single list, it would fill a large volume. The list would include a great many familiar occupations—geologists, x-ray technicians, science teachers, social security administrators, and agronomists—but it would also catalogue some of the most unusual or advanced skills. It should not be forgotten that, although we are mainly discussing over-all organization in this chapter, aid always works through persons.

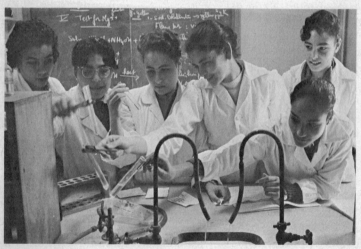

Students at work in the chemistry laboratory of the University of Alexandria's Higher Institute of Nursing, Egypt, established with the assistance of WHO.

One expert, sent to Thailand by the International Atomic Energy Agency, found himself feeding radio-active meat to cobras. He was a specialist in the medical application of radio-isotopes which, in this case, were being used in the study of snake venoms and their antidotes, in a country where snake bites are a serious hazards.

Two of his colleagues were sent to "wash gold" in Madagascar. They are training prospectors in the technique of exploring for surface gold and, at the same time, are helping to organize a cooperative for gold prospectors in that island, where gold exports are important.

An FAO expert went to the Sudan in 1958 to teach a highly-specialized cultivation process to Sudanese "shell farmers". He showed them, first, how to collect the larvae, place them on bamboo frames, and then deposit them in an underwater nursery, protected by a cover of wirenetting. He was thus sowing for future cultivation a species of valuable pearl-bearing shellfish which was threatened with extinction.

In this way the names of the various members of the United Nations family are already familiar titles all across the globe. But

The economy of Libya is based on agriculture and the raising of livestock, and since 1952 a team of FAO experts have been helping these services.

"FAO" and "WHO", and so on, are a great deal more than labels. They are becoming daily more effective in presenting to millions of ordinary people a new technique of diplomacy—a diplomacy of world service, whose flag is the blue ensign of the United Nations and whose loyalty is directed towards all the human race.

The next chapter will carry this concept into further areas of technical assistance, as practised by the Specialized Agencies we have just enumerated, and later chapters will describe the role of the World Bank and the Special Fund in these expanding operations. But it might be useful at this point to review briefly the part that the Specialized Agencies are playing in the joint enterprise that is now designated as the "Development Decade".

TOWARDS A COMMON CAMPAIGN

All these agencies and programmes (and others not specifically mentioned above) have responded to the challenge of the "gap" within the limits of their own functions and funds. In the general field of education UNESCO, for instance, has rapidly shaped its policies to meet the challenge by giving direct assistance not only in designated fields of education as such, but also in the natural and social sciences, cultural activities, and mass-communication. Likewise, the services of ILO, with nearly a half-century of such experience, have been increasingly put at the disposal of the "new" nations—especially in regard to the vital training programmes affecting the work force as a whole. FAO has long provided Governments with specialists in such fields as nutrition, fisheries and animal disease control, as we have seen. WHO teams have checked outbreaks of cholera in the Middle East, started a world-wide anti-malaria campaign—and actually increased human longevity, thus adding, incidentally, to the tasks of some of its sister agencies, such as FAO.

Yet this kind of *ad hoc* action was seen to be totally inadequate in facing the immense and increasing calls being made from all quarters on the United Nations system of mutual aid. Hence, in 1949, the UN "expanded" programme began. Ten years later, in 1959, international assistance for economic development took another step forward when the United Nations Special Fund was set up to help needy countries to lay the groundwork of a more

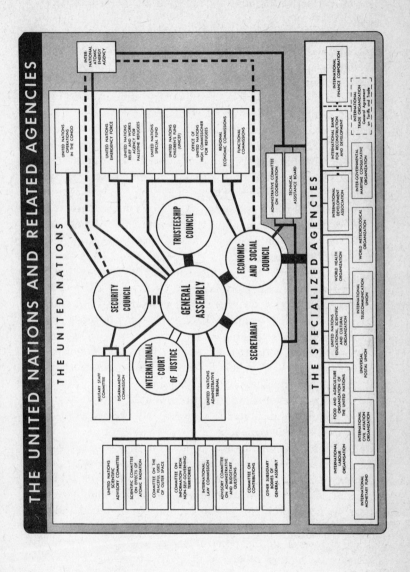

THE UNITED NATIONS AND RELATED AGENCIES

THE UNITED NATIONS

INTER-NATIONAL ATOMIC ENERGY AGENCY

UNITED NATIONS OPERATIONS IN THE CONGO

UNITED NATIONS EMERGENCY FORCE

UNITED NATIONS RELIEF AND WORKS AGENCY FOR PALESTINE REFUGEES

UNITED NATIONS SPECIAL FUND

UNITED NATIONS CHILDREN'S FUND (UNICEF)

OFFICE OF UNITED NATIONS HIGH COMMISSIONER FOR REFUGEES

REGIONAL ECONOMIC COMMISSIONS

FUNCTIONAL COMMISSIONS

ADMINISTRATIVE COMMITTEE ON COORDINATION

TECHNICAL ASSISTANCE BOARD

TRUSTEESHIP COUNCIL

SECURITY COUNCIL

GENERAL ASSEMBLY

ECONOMIC AND SOCIAL COUNCIL

SECRETARIAT

INTERNATIONAL COURT OF JUSTICE

MILITARY STAFF COMMITTEE

DISARMAMENT COMMISSION

UNITED NATIONS ADMINISTRATIVE TRIBUNAL

UNITED NATIONS SCIENTIFIC ADVISORY COMMITTEE

SCIENTIFIC COMMITTEE ON EFFECTS OF ATOMIC RADIATION

COMMITTEE ON THE PEACEFUL USES OF OUTER SPACE

COMMITTEE ON INFORMATION FROM NON-SELF-GOVERNING TERRITORIES

INTERNATIONAL LAW COMMISSION

ADVISORY COMMITTEE ON ADMINISTRATIVE AND BUDGETARY QUESTIONS

COMMITTEE ON CONTRIBUTIONS

OTHER SUBSIDIARY BODIES OF GENERAL ASSEMBLY

THE SPECIALIZED AGENCIES

INTERNATIONAL FINANCE CORPORATION

INTERNATIONAL TRADE ORGANIZATION General Agreement on Tariffs and Trade

INTERNATIONAL BANK FOR RECONSTRUCTION AND DEVELOPMENT

INTER-GOVERNMENTAL MARITIME CONSULTATIVE ORGANIZATION

INTERNATIONAL DEVELOPMENT ASSOCIATION

WORLD METEOROLOGICAL ORGANIZATION

WORLD HEALTH ORGANIZATION

INTERNATIONAL TELECOMMUNICATION UNION

UNITED NATIONS EDUCATIONAL, SCIENTIFIC AND CULTURAL ORGANIZATION

UNIVERSAL POSTAL UNION

FOOD AND AGRICULTURE ORGANIZATION OF THE UNITED NATIONS

INTERNATIONAL CIVIL AVIATION ORGANIZATION

INTERNATIONAL LABOUR ORGANISATION

INTERNATIONAL MONETARY FUND

effective *capital investment*—as we shall examine more fully in Chapter 6.

Since then, the pace has greatly quickened. The newest link in this chain of aid through the United Nations is the International Development Association, established in 1960. As will be explained in Chapter 5, the IDA enables large-scale and long-term loans to be granted to increase productivity, aimed at raising standards of living in the less-developed areas.

To take a concrete example, the Special Fund concentrates on getting rid of the obstacles to the progress of a country or region, by making possible surveys of natural resources, manpower, skills and industrial possibilities, so that a *factual* basis can be for planned economic advance. The need for such surveys is primary and becomes clearer every day. "The fundamental prerequisite for rational development of natural resources anywhere in the world" states a recent United Nations report on economic development, "is a mass of factual knowledge recorded in an immediately useable form. What is the extent of the territory and how many people live in it? How much of the land is cultivable and for what kinds of crops? Where must new highways or railways be built, or harbours, or airports? Are there any deposits of minerals that could be extracted and used? Is there water enough, on the surface or underground, for the firms and factories that will one day need it? Where is the energy to come from that must drive the machines of an expanding economy? These are some of the most elementary questions; hundreds of others, more specific, detailed and difficult to answer, will arise at every stage of a country's development".[5]

One of the great advantages which this growing network of assistance possesses is that "it can draw on a world-wide pool of experience and technical knowledge in many diverse fields and a range of contacts which are unparalleled, if they can be brought to bear upon the problems of each country in a unified and swift manner. The services offered by it are impartial and without political strings or implications. It has no vested interest in specific sectors as against others, or in specific types of development or in specific projects for financing . . . By their constitutional

---

[5] *Natural Resources* (Volume II of "*Science and Technology for Development*" series) United Nations, New York, 1963.

procedures, the United Nations organizations act only on the requests of Governments, although their advice and suggestions are independent of Governments".[6]

THE DEVELOPMENT DECADE IS BORN

Nevertheless, it was the growing recognition that all the national and international efforts thus far made had still not narrowed the gap, which led to the decision of the United Nations General Assembly in 1961 to inaugurate the "Development Decade." The Decade aims, in short, at the all-round growth of the economic structure of each less-developed country so as to attain a substantial and continuing increase in the standard of living of its population. Each country has been invited to set its own target or series of targets. It is too early yet to assess the full progress of this all-purpose campaign, but it is undoubtedly the biggest venture in world economic cooperation ever attempted in man's history.[7]

"The United National General Assembly issued a call to the conscience of mankind when it labelled the decade of the 1960's a UN Decade of Development—a decade in which to make major inroads against hunger, poverty, ignorance, and disease". Thus Paul G. Hoffman welcomed the campaign in his *World Without Want*; and he summed up its principal aim as follows: "The Assembly set as its goal a 5 per cent increase each year in the aggregate income of the developing countries. This may seem high, since in the 1950's the average yearly increase was only slightly over 3 per cent, but it is a necessary goal."

We might take a step further this point about the "5 per cent increase"—which, be it noted, is a *minimum* figure. The Secretary-General stated in the report, cited above:

> "We are begining to understand the real aims of development and the nature of the development process. We are learning that development concerns not only man's material needs, but also the improvement of the social conditions of his life and his broad human aspirations. Development is not just economic growth, it is growth plus change. As our understanding of development deepens, it may prove possible

---

[6] *The United Nations Development Decade—Proposals for Action,* (E/3613), United Nations, New York, 1962.
[7] The General Assembly Resolution is reproduced as *Appendix 1.*

27

in the developing countries to compress stages of growth through which the developed countries have passed. It may also be necessary to examine afresh the methods by which the goals of development may be attained."[8]

This means that new methods of international cooperation, added to those already well tried, will have to be employed in order to take full advantage of the economic and technological procedures which have emerged in recent years. This exploration into fresh territory has formed the substance of several United Nations conferences of late, not least the Geneva Conferences in 1963 and 1964 dealing, respectively, with science and world trade.

The central economic objective of the Decade is, as stated above, to create conditions in which the national incomes of the developing countries will increase by *at least* 5 per cent annually by the year 1970, and continue to expand thereafter. If this can be accomplished—even if the population of the developing countries continues to rise at its present rate of 2 to 2½ per cent yearly —it is believed that personal living standards can be doubled within about 25 years. If, however, the growth of population should be more rapid by the end of the decade than it is now, the raising of living standards will take correspondingly longer.

Nevertheless, the first objective for 1970 is within our reach, given a greater willingness to make the efforts and sacrifices required. If achieved, it would open up for a significant number of less-developed countries the prospect of a real improvement in the conditions of life of their peoples. It offers especially a great hope for the young men and women living today, who will be the nations of tomorrow.

It is clear that this kind of approach to development implies planning of each national economy; not planning in isolation— along the lines of national autarchy, which was so lamentable an experience in Europe during the inter-War years—but planning in relation to the whole range of international assistance. "During the Development Decade", runs a United Nations survey of the problem, "the United Nations family proposes to give high priority to intensifying assistance to any under-developed country which asks for it, both in formulating a sound develop-

---

[8] *op. cit.*

28

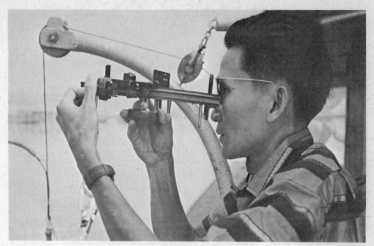

A young Lao engineer working with the Canadian Survey team, which is conducting a survey of the Mekong River, as recommended by a United Nations survey mission.

ment plan and in carrying it out through the mobilization of its own resources and the enlistment of the necessary supplementary aid and co-operation from abroad. Action to this end can be conceived in four stages: first, help in the collection of the necessary basic information; second, help in the establishment of effective planning machinery and the elaboration of sound planning methods appropriate to the conditions obtaining in the country concerned; third, help in working out the plan; and, lastly, assistance in implementing the plan".[9]

The heart of the problem of stepped-up development on the scale now being demanded lies, therefore, in the setting up of defined targets by each individual country. Each Government has to determine its specific national objectives, as well as the difficulties to be overcome, and what it considers its development "potential" to be. Such an objective, to be successful, involves the mobilization of the human resources of the nation as a whole. This stress on human resources is a precondition for achieving the material aims of the Development Decade. In fact, "the un-utilized talents of their people constitute the chief present waste,

[9] *Science and Planning* (Vol. VII of *Conference on Science and Technology for Development* series) UN, New York, 1963.

and the chief future hope, of the developing countries," runs the Secretary-General's report previously referred to; and, as a consequence, "high priority must accordingly be given to establishing educational systems well adapted to the economic and social needs of the development countries."[10]

NEW METHODS: NEW ATTITUDES

Leaving aside this basic question of educating an entire generation to play its part in the Development Decade—a topic which is dealt with in some detail in *Education and Training*—it is obvious that "new methods" must involve new attitudes on the part of the developed, as well as the developing peoples. As regards the former, some recent observations of the noted international economist, Gunnar Myrdal, are again appropriate:

> "When international aid becomes unilateral and politics thus enters into its distribution, both moral and economic standards are apt to crumble. A selection according to political interests is often bound to imply the diversion of aid to the less needy countries or to those least capable of using it effectively for economic advancement.
>
> "In the receiving countries, unilateral aid may have equally unfortunate effects. The political conditions of the aid are resented by their peoples. Indeed, political strings and the existence of ulterior motives will be suspected, even when they are not present."[11]

Similarly, a distinguished American authority has admitted the glaring imperfections of such aid and has pointed out that, "two decades of experience have failed to produce agreement on a general theory of foreign assistance—any more than they have given foreign aid a reliable basis of political support or developed clear guidelines for success in the field. Yet foreign aid has become an accepted instrument of foreign policy, and it is indispensable that we understand better what it can and cannot do."[12]

Returning, therefore, to the requirements facing the developing countries themselves, a number of radical approaches have

10 *Education and Training* (Vol. VI of *Conference on Science and Technology for Development* series) United Nations, New York, 1963.
11 Gunnar Myrdal: *Challenge to Affluence*, Pantheon Books, New York, 1963.
12 Arthur Schlesinger, Jr., in *The New York Times Book Review*, 2 May 1964.

30

been emerging from their response to the Development Decade, which can be summed up under the following general heads:

(1) *National Planning has become the No. 1 essential.* One-time objections to planning, largely attributable to a misunderstanding of the role envisaged for the private sector in most development plans, have almost wholly disappeared from the literature of the Development Decade. It is generally accepted that the basic purpose of a national development plan is to provide a programme of *action* for the achievement of specific targets, based on factual studies of the resources available. This is not merely a question of stating aims, but of translating national objectives into action programmes.

(2) *Detailed knowledge of national resources is basic.* The United Nations Special Fund, as stated above, has concentrated its efforts on "pre-investment" work, giving special attention to producing studies of natural resources, in addition to promoting technical and vocational training of a nation's "human's resources" and the establishment of institutions of applied research. (See Chapter 5.)

(3) *Outside Capital assistance is indispensable.* A necessity of national growth, capital assistance is also one of the most valuable expressions of international solidarity. It is claimed that, if such assistance could reach a level of even 1 per cent of the national incomes of the advanced countries during the Decade—as accepted unanimously in principle by the United Nations General Assembly—it would represent a major contribution to the success of the Decade.

(4) *Expert personnel must be brought in.* The shortages of highly skilled personnel, rather than a shortage of material resources or finance, is now seen as the greatest obstacle to planned national action. Foreign experts from the advanced countries should, in setting up institutions, train national personnel to take over their own work when they have to leave.

(5) *Human resources have cardinal importance.* The widening of the people's horizons through general education, plus practical training, is a precondition of long-term national development. The total number of trained people in the developing countries must be increased by at least 10 per cent *per year*, if the economic objectives of the Decade are to be achieved.

A SWITCH TO BE MADE

No survey of the factors shaping the Development Decade can ignore, however, the present diversion of human energy, skills, and savings from the purposes stressed above to arms production. Current expenditures on national armaments *are about equal to the aggregate national incomes of all underdeveloped countries put together, and about ten times their net capital formation.*

The United Nations was founded "to save succeeding generations from the scourge of war". Yet the world is spending about $120 billion a year on the arms race. The United States itself spends about $50 billion a year on armaments—more than half of the Federal Government's budget; in the United States the arms race costs each man, woman, and child almost $300 a year.

Some 50 to 75 million people are involved throughout the world and more than 20,000,000 are now in military service. (In the United States more than 7 million people are absorbed in defense efforts, including over two million in the armed forces.) Yet, in spite of these mammoth efforts, national security shrinks with the perfection of each new weapon, since each new weapon is so fast and so powerful that adequate protection cannot be developed to defend against it. Each new invention makes present defense measures out-of-date.

Obviously, this is not the place to discuss disarmament policies as such; but it is relevant to our purpose that, by another unanimous General Assembly declaration in 1953, the world's governments have agreed to devote a portion of the savings achieved through internationally-supervised world-wide disarmament to an international fund, within the framework of the United Nations, "to assist the development and reconstruction" of these needy countries. The fulfillment of this pledge would, in itself, go a long way towards providing the outside capital assistance so desperately required for the goals of the Decade. There is nothing "impossible" about the objectives of the Decade—it is a question of intention, of *will*.

Moreover, it was pointed out at the 1963 Geneva Conference on Science and Technology for Development that there had been little organized effort to bring science and technology specifically to bear upon the particular problems of under-development. The increasing burden of these non-economic armaments had made it far more difficult to direct scientific and technological leadership and resources to the problems of the developing countries. Heavy financial aid, modern equipment, and skilled personnel, which might otherwise be devoted to the latter's problems, were pre-empted by the arms race between the Great Powers. It has been estimated that the required acceleration in the growth of the aggregate incomes in the developing countries from 3½ per cent to 5 per cent would necessitate the diversion of no more than 10 per cent of the savings that would result from a halving of present armament expenditures.

Finally, a recent United Nations expert report on the *Economic and Social Consequences of Disarmament,* introduces a further consideration bearing on the long-term interests of the less-developed areas. It warns that, since "the competing claims in developing countries are also urgent, there is a serious possibility that the financial resources released by disarmament might be rapidly absorbed by purely national aims. It is therefore desirable that an appropriate proportion of these resources should be allocated to international aid in its various forms, simultaneously with their use for domestic purposes."[13]

THE BETTER LIFE

Lest it should be assumed that the problems of the Decade, to which we have devoted this chapter, are essentially material or organizational, due weight should be given to the personal emphasis which constantly marks the experience of the United Nations family of agencies and its devoted servants. The words of a former Director-General of the UN Technical Assistance Administration, Hugh L. Keenleyside, come to mind: "The chief concern of those who administer the technical assistance program is priority in peoples rather than in governments. The latter are agencies through which the aid is channeled, but it is the men and women and children who are the final recipients who are the real objects of our concern."

Similarly, the Director-General of the ILO, David Morse, told the 1963 Geneva conference: "Economic growth is not an end in itself, but an indispensable means towards the real end—a better

---

[13] *Economic and Social Consequences of Disarmament* (E/3593) United Nations, New York, 1963.

A student of carpentry at work under a Palestinian instructor at the Clerical and Technical Training Centre, Tripoli, Libya, where experts from both UNESCO and ILO conduct classes.

life in a good society." And he continued: "Economic growth has to be considered as a function of a wider process of social reconstruction. In this there are two other indispensable elements. One is greater material well-being for the population as a whole, and particularly for workers and their families. The other—and perhaps of the three the most important of all—is opportunity for the development of the individual personality and for the growth of institutions through which people can freely and responsibly decide the goals for which they are prepared to work."[14]

This concept of "the better life" was emphatically endorsed by the late President John F. Kennedy, when he addressed the United Nations General Assembly, for the last time, on 20th September, 1963:

> "Never before has man had such capacity to control his own environment—to end thirst and hunger—to conquer poverty and disease—to banish illiteracy and massive human misery. We have the power to make this the best generation of mankind in the history of the world—or to make it the last."

1310105

---

[14] *Education and Training* (Vol. VI of *Conference on Science and Technology for Development* series), United Nations, New York, 1963.

3

Mutual Aid Makes Sense

"Underdeveloped countries suffer from a paralyzing lack of capital, which is the fulcrum of production—capital in the shape of ploughs, tools, engines, cranes, factories, warehouses, dams. Without capital, a man is limited to what he can produce with his ingenuity and the strength of his bare hands, plus the most primitive equipment—stick ploughs, ox-carts, hand-dug irrigation ditches, hand-turned spinning wheels." Thus Paul G. Hoffman, Managing-Director of the United Nations Special Fund, epitomised the central problem which faces all developing countries alike.[1]

Archimedes said: "Give me a place to stand on, and my fulcrum will raise the earth." United Nations assistance to these countries is providing that "place to stand on" for the "fulcrum of production" to raise the standards of two-thirds of the human race still living in want.

But, to realize their development aims, low-income countries require more than financial help. They also need guidance in formulating and carrying out sound development projects. It is in this area, namely, the transfer of the *capacity* to create wealth and well-being, that the United Nations is performing a key function.

Over the years, the United Nations system has built up a body of knowledge and experience offering the highest guarantee of impartiality and understanding. Today, governments may seek and do receive aid from the United Nations to meet almost any

---

[1] Paul G. Hoffman: *World Without Want,* Harper and Row, New York, 1962.

36

conceivable problem in the economic and social fields. This aid ranges from demonstrating ways of raising better cattle to the art of using radioisotopes in industry and medicine. The United Nations services to the advancing peoples of the earth stretch all the way from child and maternity training to the actual financing of large-scale industrial projects. In the following three chapters, the particular functions of the United Nations Programme of Technical Assistance, the World Bank, and the Special Fund will be examined in turn; but in this chapter some background prin-

Students are attending classes for the first time under a UNESCO fundamental education officer in the High Andes.

ciples may help to make clear the fundamental differences between United Nations aid programmes and some of the forms of unilateral "foreign aid" practised by powerful and wealthy nations in their own right.

The strength of the United Nations system lies in the fact that it has at its disposal a diversity of resources and models on which it can draw, and it has gained wide experience in applying them to countries at very different stages of development. Since the recipient country itself is a member of the organization dispensing the aid, and often provides its own experts for the benefit of other countries, the distinction between donor and recipient is minimized. Thus, the benefiting country has the feeling of "sharing" in a common venture in which it is itself a full partner.

OUTSIDE THE UNITED NATIONS SYSTEM

It is not surprising, however, that the United Nations does not stand alone in recognizing the needs of less-developed peoples. A common awareness throughout the world of the need for co-operation between peoples for the advance of human progress has produced a number of channels through which these countries can generate or receive help. A brief sketch of some of these must suffice for our present purpose; though it must be understood that no assessment of foreign aid programmes can be attempted here, except in so far as it relates to the general topic of this book.

First, as is well known, governments in the developed countries have given and continue to give money, resources, and skills on a direct country-to-country basis. (More detailed reference to this point is made below.) The same governments participate in regional undertakings, which provide regular assistance to their members. The Commonwealth, headed by Great Britain, has sponsored the South-East Asian "Colombo Plan", created in 1950, and the Organization of American States provides similar assistance to the Americas.

Secondly, private industrial concerns in developed countries have established branches of their industries in less-developed countries, thereby supplying needed capital investment, as well as local employment opportunities. Some industrial concerns in advanced countries arrange training schemes at home, to which they invite participants from the less-developed countries.

Thirdly, valuable assistance to less-developed countries is provided by non-governmental organizations. Private organizations in developed countries, such as youth groups and schools, have "adopted" villages or other small communities in developing countries and provided assistance to them in a number of ways. Professional and labour associations encourage the exchange of skills and technical knowledge through international conferences and also through the exchange of experts.

Fourthly, organizations like the International Committee of

38

the Red Cross and the League of Red Cross Societies, with its many national Red Cross and Red Crescent Societies, provide emergency aid upon which all countries can call in time of need. Non-governmental bodies which work at the international level, such as the YMCA and the YWCA, have been responsible for some useful assistance projects.

A BALANCED PICTURE

Since the present book is devoted to the United Nations development programme, no detailed account can be given of these and other "outside" sources of help. Nevertheless, a balanced picture of international technical assistance would have to give due weight to what has been done and is still being done by bilateral and multilateral assistance of this variety.[2]

When the member states of the United Nations unanimously proclaimed the 1960's the "Development Decade", each member Government was, in effect, acknowledging its *individual* responsibility to promote the economic and social advancement of the developing countries, as laid down in the Charter. It was, of course, recognized that the primary duty rested with the governments of the developing countries themselves for the will and the resources needed to achieve their stated goals of improved living standards. However, the advanced countries were clearly obligated to ensure the success of these self-help efforts by themselves providing such requisites as capital, equipment, and technical *know-how*.

In fulfilling their share of this responsibility, the governments of the less-developed nations are naturally spending large sums for their own development. Nevertheless, the assistance these countries are receiving from outside in funds, goods and services has been estimated recently at about $8,500,000,000 a year. About one-third of this amount consists of private investment; while the remaining $6 billion represents the public flow of economic and social aid, through bilateral and multilateral arrangements.

It is estimated that about *10 per cent* of this flow of public funds is channelled annually through the United Nations family

[2] See *Technical Assistance Newsletter,* No. 19, 1963, United Nations (New York), for a general survey of these kinds of assistance.

for international technical assistance, for loans by the World Bank and its affiliates, and for such schemes as the World Food Programme. This means that, at present, about 90 per cent of the public outflow is composed of the major bilateral and multilateral

Experts in conference with the U.N. Resident Technical Assistance Representative in the Philippines, which has requested United Nations technical assistance in several fields.

programmes which, up to now, has been spent outside the United Nations system.

The economic assistance given, for example, by the United States Government to the developing countries accounts for more than one-half of all global assistance rendered. It embraces the provision of grants and technical assistance by the Agency for International Development (AID), the Food-for-Peace Programme, which deals with agricultural commodities, the Export-

Import Bank and the Peace Corps. The United States also entered into an arrangement with the Food and Agriculture Organization (and may do so with other United Nations organizations) to attach a limited number of Peace Corps personnel to international missions. The individuals involved remain the administrative and financal responsbility of the Peace Corps and are not subject to United Nations regulations during the time that they work under the supervision of UN experts.

The principal share of the United States economic assistance is administered directly by AID, which received $2.6 billion in appropriations for the fiscal year 1963. Approximately 60 per cent of this amount is being used for long-term loans and the remaining 40 per cent is for non-repayable development grants, which includes technical assistance. More than half of the grants are going to the countries of Latin America (under the Alliance for Progress) and Africa. The Organization of American States is not itself a capital-providing body; but it maintains a voluntarily-financed Technical Co-operation Programme, composed of specific projects, for regional training centers and advanced technical instruction to trainees from all countries of the Americas.

Although United States aid programmes are represented in over 80 of the less-developed countries, four-fifths of all the assistance is concentrated in about 20 countries, the largest country programmes being the Republic of Korea, China (Formosa), the Philippines, the Republic of Vietnam, India, Pakistan, Israel, Turkey, Greece, and Brazil.

Similarly, the United Kingdom gives economic assistance principally to countries in the British Commonwealth, through development loans, grants, and various forms of technical assistance. In fiscal year 1962-63, a total of $388 million (£138 million) was spent *bilaterally* on all forms of assistance, including expenditures under the Colombo Plan. The nature of British aid ranges from the financing of specific capital projects, through the general finance of imports, to the provision in the dependent territories of funds for normal local expenditure.

Britain provides aid to developing countries through such bodies as the Commonwealth Development Corporation and the Department of Technical Co-operation. The Commonwealth Development Corporation may not be so spectacular as its American counterpart, but Britain has been in this business longer, having started in 1929. The Department of Technical Co-operation concentrates on the interchange of human contacts. There are still 19,000 British men and women serving in the developing countries under the British Government's umbrella, and about 50,000 students from these countries are in Britain learning the skills needed to enable them to pilot their own way forward.

The French bilateral programme, like the US and the British, includes the provision of development loans, grants, and technical assistance; but its emphasis at the present time is preponderantly on grants. Assistance is given almost entirely to countries in the franc area. The division of French aid, geographically, would show the greatest share going to Algeria; the next largest to the 14 independent African States, and to the group of countries comprised of Morocco, Tunisia, Cambodia, Laos and Vietnam; as well as to the French Overseas Departments and Territories.

A MODEST STREAM

The effect of this global sum on the economies of the developing nations under review is beyond the scope of this book; least of all can we appraise its political or military overtones. But a warning not to overstress the comparison between this "outside" aid and UN aid—which is always tailored to the needs of the country requesting it—is confirmed by the following opinion of a competent observer:

> "It is indeed extremely difficult to isolate and identify that portion of Western capital and economic aid to an underdeveloped country which makes any significant contribution towards raising the material level of the mass of people living there. A few favored places with white-settler populations, like Algeria and Rhodesia, absorb an unduly large share of the capital moving out of Europe. These are not, in the nature of the case, the areas of mass poverty, where upwards of one thousand million people are pressing with increasing urgency on the means of subsistence. Into this central area of the struggle, and especially into the countries with no military commitment to the West, the broad flow of international capital and aid, which looks so impressive at the outset, is reduced to a modest stream."[3]

[3] Andrew Shonfield: *The Attack on World Poverty* (Vintage Book), Neew New York, 1964.

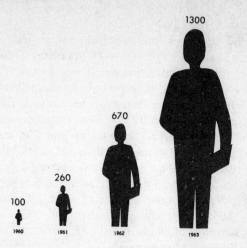

1300

670

260

100

1960 1961 1962 1963

NUMBER OF INTERNATIONAL EXPERTS SERVING IN FIELD

It is not only the West, of course, which is "in the market" as concerns foreign aid. The Government of the Union of Soviet Republics has agreements with about thirty developing countries, covering the provision of economic and technical assistance. The total amount committed for this purpose in 1962, for instance, has been estimated at approximately $400 million.

Industrial development is the main field of activity in the Soviet aid programme. Other major areas are transportation and communications, hydro-electric power projects—such as the Aswan High Dam project in Egypt—and mineral development projects. Under the agreements mentioned above, the Soviet Union has undertaken to assist the construction of over 480 industrial plants and other projects, including 32 in India, 21 in Indonesia, 50 in Afghanistan, 90 in the United Arab Republic, 73 in Iraq, 11 in Syria, 42 in Ghana, 77 in Guinea, 14 in Somalia, 10 in Mali, and 9 in the Sudan.

In most cases, the agreements lay down that the Soviet Union will provide the Governments of the countries concerned a loan with which to defray the expenses incurred by Soviet organizations in carrying out, planning, and prospecting operations, delivering equipment and materials, assisting in the assembly and operation of the equipment, training national personnel, and various other forms of technical assistance.

43

To keep the matter of communist aid in perspective, the following recent example of the entry of Mainland China into the arena is not without its significance. It can be taken as typical of what may continue to be expected. An immediate grant to Kenya of $3 million was announced from Nairobi, following an agreement signed in Peking by two Kenya ministers, after visits to Peking and Moscow. In addition to the grant "to assist Kenya regarding its present and immediate financial stress," the Chinese have also agreed to make an interest-free loan of 65 million Swiss francs (about $15 million) for development projects over the next five years. The loan will take the form of technical assistance and equipment "according to the capability of the Government of the People's Republic of China and the requirements of the Government of Kenya." Moreover, the loan is repayable over 10 years, either in the form of Kenya produce, in Swiss francs, or in any other convertible currency agreed upon by the two Governments. (The London *Times*, 20.5.64.)

Other technically advanced countries have their own systems of bilateral assistance, in addition to regional and multilateral schemes comparable to the Colombo Plan and the O.A.S., already mentioned. But further elucidation of these would take us beyond the limits of our present study. The foregoing sketch of these "outside" sources of aid has been made chiefly to give emphasis to the important considerations which follow.

CLAIMS TO UNIQUENESS

Notwithstanding the value and extent of the operations briefly outlined above, the role of the United Nations family is unique in so many ways that it can properly be regarded as operating on a different level, both qualitatively and quantitatively. Taken together, the United Nations and its many agencies provide the most widespread channel for international co-operation between virtually all countries of the world. Founded on the guiding principles of the Charter, the United Nations has given a new meaning to international aid, the long-term significance of which is not lost on the leaders of the developing nations themselves.

These principles include the right of each requesting government itself to decide what help it needs and in what form. They guarantee that technical assistance will not be used as a means of foreign political or economic interference in the internal affairs of the requesting government. Developing countries always attach much importance to the conditions associated with any assistance they receive from outside—particularly as concerns non-interference politically. These countries are naturally anxious to safeguard the prestige which belongs to them as sovereign independent states. It is essential, therefore, that they should be able to request assistance in circumstances which do not reflect on their new sense of nationhood.

Moreover, as Gunnar Myrdal observes, "an underdeveloped country may be willing and even grateful to take from an international agency the advice which it is not happy or, because of popular resentment, not able to accept under prodding by a single country, least of all when that country is very rich, powerful, and carefree in its public expressions. This is, of course, one important reason why aid is best channelled through an international agency."[4]

Then, many of the issues besetting developing countries overlap national boundaries. Their problems are often regional in character and the assistance which is most welcome must also be regional in scope. When dealing with epidemic diseases, such as malaria eradication, or with the control of locusts, it is plainly an advantage for a group of countries to co-operate in a scheme of technical assistance for dealing with their common problem.

Another type of project which lends itself to regional treatment is that concerned with the exploitation of a large river basin, where the waters flow through two or more countries. The lower Mekong River Project will be taken as an excellent example of this in later chapters. Such programmes are obviously more complicated than projects confined to a single country, since it is necessary to reconcile different national interests, and to subordinate them to the benefit of the whole region. This is obviously not a task for an "outside" government or private organization to tackle on a bilateral basis.

TO SERVE THE PEOPLE

The United Nations method makes it possible for a country or

---

[4] Gunnar Myrdal: *Challenge to Affluence*, Pantheon Books, New York, 1963.

a group of countries needing technical assistance to draw on the expertise and experience of a multitude of nations with varied kinds of economic development of their own and with differing social and cultural patterns. These programmes aim, not at influencing or controlling, but at *supplementing* the efforts of the less-developed countries to strengthen their national economies on their own terms and in their own way. Thus, they can promote their economic and political life in true independence and raise the living standards of their entire populations without being beholden to some foreign government or absentee corporation.

In fact, the general debate at the 1964 World Trade Conference (taken up in Chapter 7) brought out clearly that more and more countries under development deplored a situation which tended to put them at the mercy of contending "economic imperialisms," as they saw it.

This view was frankly presented in a recent Swarthmore Lecture, in London, by J. Duncan Wood as follows:

> "This competitive attitude to world economic development is an insult to human intelligence. To use the needs of others as a means to court favour is to court disaster. Fortunately, there are indications that the developing countries themselves will not permit the wealthier countries to continue to make political capital out of their economic predicament, or to infringe their sovereignty by offering aid on condition of accepting a particular ideological alignment. . . . Fortunately, too, the great powers themselves have so frequently announced their concern for the developing countries, that they cannot afford to offend or neglect them. It remains for them to recognize that it is in their common interest to supply the aid that is required through channels acceptable to the developing countries, namely, through multilateral institutions in which the recipients themselves can state their needs and help to determine the means by which they are met."[5]

Members of the United Nations co-operating in its programmes have explicitly agreed, as we have noted, that their own technical assistance should not be used as a means of political and economic interference in the internal affairs of countries asking for it. Furthermore, the international organizations actually providing

---

[5] J. Duncan Wood: *Building The Institutions of Peace* (Swarthmore Lecture), Allen and Unwin, London, 1962.

technical assistance must "avoid distinctions arising from the political structure of the country requesting assistance, or from the race or religion of its population".

Hence, United Nations multi-national aid has marked a significant, if not revolutionary, advance over previous procedures. As has been stressed already, help is given only at the request of a government and, as far as possible, it is given to that government in the form it desires, since the skill-sharing operations of the United Nations and its Specialized Agencies are mainly aimed at helping countries *to help themselves.*

A team of technical aid experts are sent to a country to train its people to take their own place at the earliest moment. There can be no "possessiveness" about the United Nations approach— the emissaries of the United Nations are there to serve the people of the country, not themselves. Nor is UN technical assistance designed to impose internal changes or "reforms" on those seeking aid; least of all to gain the support of the needy country for the political or military objectives of a foreign power. This "neutralization" of international economies has been aptly expressed by D.C. Coyle as follows:

> "Under the UN flag, men can go on a mission with men of other nations to do a job that plainly gives them these creative satisfactions. The same satisfactions are, to be sure, common among the technicians who work for the United States Point Four Program or the Colombo Plan, or for one of the private foundations. But in places where the people are keenly suspicious of the Great Powers, the same technicians can go under UN auspices and be more readily accepted."[6]

A TWO-WAY STREET

Another uniqueness of these international programmes—"supranational" might be a better term—is that those who receive aid may, and often do, provide aid to others as well. Experience has shown that nearly every country, regardless of the stage of its development, can provide some special knowledge or skill to help some other country to improve its own living standards. This is because, as stated above, the United Nations programmes tap

---

[6] D. C. Coyle: *The United Nations and How It Works,* a Mentor Book, York, 1964.

not just the skills of the few—the more developed—nations, but a universal reservoir made up of the technical experience of every member nation of the United Nations family. Such programmes are not a one-way flow of skills from the more to the less-developed countries; they are rather a cross-fertilization of skills, which is world-wide in its operation.

An example of this came to light recently when an African government invited an expert from a highly-developed country to train its people in the use of calculating machinery, so as to compile its first national census. An office full of obsolete machinery confronted the foreign expert and rendered his task impossible. The United Nations later sent a statistician from a neighbouring country, who had dealt with similar problems and who spoke the same language; he was familiar with the equipment provided, and he succeeded because he approached the task in terms of the country he was sent to help.

Under such programmes as these an expert from France has given technical training to industrial workers in Brazil; a Brazilian specialist has, in turn, been sent to Ecuador to undertake a soils survey; an Ecuadorean doctor has been lent to India to help train maternal and child health nurses; an Indian biochemist has been assigned to Iraq; and an Iraqi educator has been allocated to an adult education project in Libya. And so the cross-fertilization expands with its own success.

The programmes we have been describing can be termed "mutual aid" activities in that all members of the United Nations— the less-developed as well as the more developed—have an equal say in *shaping* them and in devising the best administrative machinery for their operation. As the diagram shows (p. 25), the technical assistance administration operates under the Economic and Social Council, which reports publicly to the General Assembly. There is thus an accountability to the world organization, which is a guarantee of the highest order.

Finally, the programmes are "mutual" in that all member governments contribute to the operating expenses. They do this partly through their regular membership dues; but most of the contributions they make to meet the operating costs of technical assistance are voluntary. These voluntary contributions pay for what is called the *Expanded* Programme of Technical Assistance

—the funds of which are shared between the United Nations and the nine international agencies which take part in the Expanded Programme.

A UNIVERSAL CONCEPT

It becomes evident that, as United Nations assistance throws up its own techniques, a new structure of world co-operation is emerging, creating its own *rationale* of collective responsibility, which carries us far from those increasingly suspect notions of "foreign aid" which dominate the thinking of most orthodox politicians. The United Nations has ushered in a universal concept, which demands not only the funds to sustain it, but a new philosophy to inspire it.*

The truth is that there is less and less room today for the condescending attitude which assumes that the "haves" are superior to the "have-nots" by natural right—that any aid they persuade themselves to render the latter is essentially an act of political charity. Indeed, some countries which are the sources of assistance for the less-developed countries are themselves shifting their motivations—and for various reasons. Let us briefly review some of them, before concluding this chapter.

Firstly, there is a growing recognition, heightened by the unmistakeable internationalism of the Twentieth Century, that the material welfare of all mankind is bound together. In the long run, everything depends on there being adequate living standards for *all* peoples. On a scientifically shrinking planet, poverty anywhere becomes a threat to prosperity everywhere. Thus, the wealthier peoples are coming to recognize that, since their own existence is linked with the well-being of the rest of mankind, improving the lot of their fellows in less-developed countries indirectly favours them too. Moreover, as an African delegate pointed out during the 1964 World Trade Conference, "the prosperity of the developed countries has to a large extent

---

* *Where Did Your Money Go—The Foreign Aid Story,* by Andrew Tully and Milton Britten (Simon & Schuster), 1964, carries this point much further by analysing factually, with a wealth of examples, what the authors describe as "the bungles, blunders, frivolities or failures in the unbelievably lavish distribution of more than 100 billion dollars of U.S. taxpayers' money from 1946 to 1963"; and is, indirectly, a powerful argument for the United Nations alternative advanced in the present book.

been built on the natural resources of the developing countries; and it was now a universally accepted principle that the strong should help and not bully the weak."

Secondly, and more important perhaps, the advanced countries are compelled to seek new ways of improving their own economies by the expansion of trade and the cultivation of new markets. In assisting the less-developed countries to plan *their* economies and raise *their* living standards, and thus to create new demands for their own goods and services, they stand to gain themselves by sharing increasingly in these overseas markets. "Without universal expansion", another delegate at the 1964 Conference pointed out, "it is not possible for 'the affluent society' to continue."

"As development proceeds", foresees Paul G. Hoffman: "certain manufacturers in the industrially advanced nations will have to meet new and stiffer competition. The Great Powers will lose the control over poorer nations that they once exercised through the purse strings. They may find themselves outvoted in world forums. They will have to learn to survive rebuffs and setbacks without modifying their essential principles and without panic."[7]

Not least, is the modern acceptance, as a working rule of international conduct, of the moral responsibility laid upon all human beings to help each other to live the good life. The United Nations Charter expresses that responsibility in precise and concrete terms. The application of this principle on a world-wide scale, and the willingness of so many countries to take part in mutual assistance programmes, has rightly been called "the shining hope of the Twentieth Century."

---

[7] Paul G. Hoffman: *World Without Want*, Harper and Row, New York, 1963.

4

Technical Assistance To The Rescue

Until 1960, Lalla Mimouna was a sleepy village of 3,000 inhabitants situated in the Gharb region of the Province of Rabat, about 100 miles to the north-east of Morocco's capital. It was surrounded by overgrown cactus underbrush, infested by snakes, posing a constant threat to both the villagers and their scant cattle. Only one passable road connected the village with the outside world and the nearest market place at Souk El Arba.

The villagers, weavers and small merchants, lived and worked in shabby shacks, suffocatingly hot in summer under the African sun and offering inadequate protection against the rain and humidity during the winter. Illiteracy was almost universal; a dilapidated hut served as a school for 20 boys. The soil was poor and the great distance from the big city market made it difficult for the weavers to compete with producers from more favourably located places.

The story of the awakening of Lalla Mimouna and its integration into the life of the nation goes back to late 1957, when a four-man United Nations "task force" arrived in Morocco at the invitation of the Government to help set up a Community Development Programme for the country. The first two years were spent reviewing the situation with officials of all levels. The outcome of the various proposals presented by the experts, on the basis of several studies and investigations, was a decision taken by the Government to the effect that a community development pilot project should be launched. The village of Lalla Mimouna became the site of the project and, in a wider sense, a microcosm of the United Nations way to self-development through international co-operation.

Later, other experts from United Nations specialized agencies came to give advice and assistance during various stages of the programme. The project was planned as a common undertaking of the Government, the United Nations, and the villagers themselves. By August 1960, things had started to roll. The first work in the village was destructive in nature: four decayed and crumbling hovels were torn down, to be replaced by new four-family houses. This was followed by the construction of 50 stores, replacing the shabby premises of the local merchants.

Another initial job was the replacement of 29 weavers' workshops. At the same time, the land in the immediate vicinity of the village was cleared of thick overgrown cactus bush. The first stage not only gave the village a new look, but gained the confidence of the inhabitants and secured their full co-operation in later projects. A survey of needs led to a community house, followed by two flour mills and three garages to shelter the trucks serving the merchants coming to the markets of the region.

The social life of the people was not overlooked. A Moorish cafe was erected in the village square. But perhaps the most important part of the programme was building the new school. The old shack, previously referred to as a school, was demolished. In its place a modern, airy and roomy building of eight classes was erected. For the first time all the boys and girls in the village were able to receive a basic education. The influx of youngsters of both sexes filled the school to capacity and an extension had to be considered. Soon, another project was taking shape: six dormitories for the administration employees and teachers, each unit consisting of two rooms equipped with a modern kitchen and utilities. Besides which, another school building for girls in the higher grades is under construction.

Then came a dispensary—with a nurse to be appointed in due course (nurses have to be trained first!). Next on the list—a big undertaking—was the reservoir, for water supply has always been a problem for Lalla Mimouna. With the completion of this project, dysentery, typhoid and other illnesses which have always plagued the villagers, will assuredly disappear.

Sanitary conditions were reviewed and suggestions for their improvement were made by the World Health Organization. An International Labour Organization expert advised the weavers on better methods of weaving woollen fabrics. The Food and Agriculture Organization undertook a study of better exploitation of sea and freshwater fish. A literacy campaign for adults, under an Egyptian expert supplied by UNESCO, is in the planning stage.

The village weavers have been told about the advantages of the co-operative system, and they have enthusiastically accepted the idea of a co-operative for the manufacture and distribution of woollen fabrics. A similar step has been taken by the small merchants, who have pooled their trucks to economise on transportation to and from the market. Additional co-operatives will soon be established for the dairy industry, fishing and farm produce.

And the *cost* of the transformation of this small world?

Up to the end of April 1963, the Government and the local administration had spent the equivalent of about $35,000, while the share of the population itself amounted to the equivalent of $85,000. The cost to the United Nations for the expert assistance, provided over several years, has been less than $75,000.

In all these improvements, the people of Lalla Mimouna have been actively involved through their village Council and other community institutions, learning to practice social democracy. And other Moroccan communities are following suit.

HOW SKILL-SHARING WORKS

Given that Lalla Mimouna is a tiny place, set against such a crowded canvas of world need, one can see in capsule form the basic elements of the vast though silent revolution of our times. The efforts of the people themselves are united with those of their leaders to raise their economic and social standards; and these efforts have been supported by the world community, by providing the elements they most need of skill, experience and, above all, unquestioned integrity.

The experts who came to Lalla Mimouna had arrived from other lands under the United Nations Expanded Technical Assistance Programme, a programme which actually goes back to 1949, as we have seen. The rapid growth of that programme and the principles on which it works, form the subject-matter of this chapter. The chief point to bear in mind is that the less-developed countries need not only money and machines for eco-

53

nomic and social betterment, but also manpower with the proper *know-how* for using them—whether they be simple scythes, complicated generators, or adding machines to handle the statistics which lie behind all development policies.

It must be obvious that more and more men and women are required everywhere today in the developing areas with the specialized training to run hospitals and health services and to improve the yield of farmlands, as well as to install and to build up effective civil services. To help these countries increase the amount of *know-how* at their disposal for speeding their economic progress, the member states of the United Nations and its Specialized Agencies set up in 1949 a joint technical assistance scheme, supported by a multi-national fund. This was the beginning of modern technical assistance under the United Nations system. From this fund there may be drawn not money as money, but *skills*; and these are built into the technical assistance programmes of today.

Timber is one of Nepal's richest resources and wood is a major export to India, hence the Government started a reforestation program following a report made by FAO.

Economic development is seldom capable of quick or spectacular solution. But the results of the multilateral operations of the United Nations and its Specialized Agencies testify to its long-term effectiveness. Several different samples of this kind of basic economic and social planning might be given at this point to illustrate how varied are the requirements of the countries seeking UN aid.

In Pakistan, a United Nations team of engineers were given responsibility for the final stages of construction of the Gudda Barrage, inaugurated in March 1963, which will irrigate nearly three million acres of land and increase food yield by an expected fifty million tons a year.

In Peru, a team of experts helped the Government recently to turn an unused airfield into a fully operational secondary airport, with a training school which is supplying recruits for the national airlines.

In Mexico, international assistance in support of national efforts has brought malaria eradication within sight. Similarly, in Mexico and Central America, four years of work by scientists and technicians, aided by a FAO expert, have controlled the locust plague by measures which prevent the insects from swarming.

In Jordan, a tanning plant was planned by one United Nations expert and designed by another and it now employs 220 workers and produces processed skins to meet internal demands, as well as for export.

In Burma and other countries of the Far East, many of the men who repair and maintain diesel engines are graduates of a training centre which technical assistance experts helped to organize. Since 1961, the Burmese Government has taken over the operation of the Diesel Centre, which has already been responsible for the training of some 200 technicians from nine Asian countries.

In the fifteen years that projects like these and thousands of others have been carried out by the Technical Assistance programme, governments have benefitted from and respected the principles which underlie not only the Expanded Programme, but all related UN activities in the economic and social field.

WHAT OF THE COST?

One promising sign of the value which governments have come to set on this type of international skill-sharing is to be found in the steadily increasing number and size of government contributions to the Expanded Programme of Technical Assistance. Fifty-four governments pledged the equivalent of just over

$20 million for the first financial period of eighteen months, ending December 31, 1951. Over 105 governments promised some $51 million between them for the year 1964. In the last fourteen years, governments have paid or pledged some $450 million. The fact that so many voluntary contributions continue to be made is proof of the regard in which the system is held throughout the world.

For reasons which will be apparent later, it is more useful to consider the current finances of the Expanded Programme and the Special Fund together. Pledges received to date (and those still expected from governments) towards the 1964 activities of the United Nations Expanded Programme and the Special Fund show an anticipated record total of $132 million for the two aid programmes coming from 108 governments. This total of $132 million includes an anticipated United States contribution for 1964 of $59 million, based on the "matching" formula under which the United States has provided 40 per cent of the total annual contributions of all governments.

Of the anticipated $132 million, approximately $51 million was pledged for the Expanded Programme of Technical Assistance and just over $80 million for the Special Fund. It should be remembered, of course, that the *regular* technical assistance activities of the United Nations family are not included in these figures; they form part of the normal budgets of the organisations concerned.

A final point might be made to the effect that, although the $132 million total represents an increase over previous years, it is still (at the moment) below the General Assembly target of $150 million for 1964. The executive heads of both programmes have continued to seek additional support from governments, with a view to reaching that minimum target.

HOW IT IS ORGANIZED

Most of the Specialized Agencies work together in providing technical aid (as mentioned in earlier chapters) whether it be paid for out of their regular budgets or out of voluntary contributions of governments in cash or services. The work of the nine Agencies that participate in the Expanded Programme, and the work of the UN itself, is co-ordinated through the body known as

PROCEDURE FOR PLANNING AND DEVELOPING THE PROGRAMME

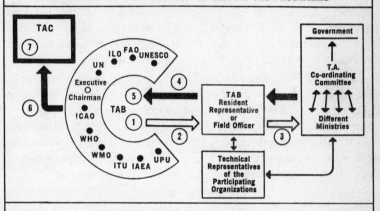

EXPLANATORY NOTES

(1) (a) TAB establishes global planning target for the field programme on the basis of probable contributions by Governments.

(b) TAB formulates target figures for country and regional programmes.

(2) Target figures communicated, via TAB Resident Representatives, to Governments.

(3) Representatives of the Participating Organizations negotiate projects with the appropriate government ministries in each country. TAB Resident Representative assists in and co-ordinates programming discussions with the Government's Technical Assistance Co-ordinating Committee, which assigns project priorities and consolidates country programme request within target figure.

(4) Governments transmit programme requests to TAB, via Resident Representatives, with copies to Participating Organizations.

(5) TAB Secretariat examines and consolidates government requests in the light of Participating Organizations' cost estimates.

(6) TAB recommends over-all programme to Technical Assistance Committee.

(7) TAC reviews and approves the over-all programme and authorizes allocation of funds for its implementation to the Participating Organizations in proportion to their shares in the approved over-all programme.

the Technical Assistance Board (TAB), on which each is represented. (See diagram.)

The World Bank and its affiliates and the International Monetary Fund have non-voting seats on the Board and co-operate in the Programme; but they do not share in Expanded Programme funds. The United Nations Children's Fund (UNICEF) also co-operates on this basis. Working closely with the Expanded Programme, the United Nations Special Fund (as will be explained in Chapter 6) helps to lay the groundwork in less-developed countries, so as to prepare the way for capital investment.

The Board is headed by an Executive Chairman. It has established field offices at the places where the work is actually being carried out. These TAB "resident representatives" serve as links between the different experts on the job and between them, their organisations, and the government ministries. They help the governments in planning the requests for Expanded Programme aid and also help evaluate such aid in their own areas.

Requests from countries needing assistance are usually submitted through the resident representatives, where such officers have been appointed, or to the chief official of the organization directly concerned. As the volume of requests greatly exceeds the resources of the Programme, requesting governments are asked to suggest their own priorities, taking into account not only their needs and resources, but also the help which they expect to receive from other programmes of external aid.

The effectiveness of this system naturally varies from country to country. It is most effective in countries in which there is already an adequate *national development plan* and where local arrangements exist for co-ordination. In countries where these conditions are lacking, the most useful task of technical assistance may often be to help the governments to overcome this lack of preliminary planning.

ROLE OF THE EXPERTS

So much for the general framework of financing and organizing technical assistance. We can now turn briefly to the personal factor involved in its field operations.

The backbone of these programmes is, of course, the experts in the field. More than 20,000 experts—of whom 13,000 were provided under the Expanded Programme—have been sent to more than 100 countries and territories on a considerable variety of schemes. In these countries, they may help to train drivers for bulldozers to turn wasteland into productive farmland; but the money to buy the bulldozers has to be obtained elsewhere—as explained in the next two chapters.

Sometimes these experts have gone out as teams to survey a country's entire economic potential, as in Haiti, Libya, or Cyprus. More often, government requests have called for the services of a single expert or a small team. They may work on such projects as the installation of a scientific laboratory, the training of statistical clerks, or the demonstration of small farm tools. Generally, however, their assistance forms part of a larger national undertaking, on which many people may be engaged. Yet the key role they play in a major government programme achieves an impact which far outweighs the modest investment of United Nations aid involved.

As stressed earlier, it would be a great mistake to assume that the experts come only from the more developed countries. Half of the countries receiving aid are already supplying experts to assist in the development of other lands. In fact, most countries nowadays have experts of their own in one or another field of economic development, though not always in sufficient numbers; and they may not always have been able to keep abreast of the latest technical advances. This brings us to the perennial question of training.

To help them acquire this new technical knowledge by study abroad, the United Nations and the Specialized Agencies provide fellowships for specialists, officials, and technicians. More than 35,000 such fellowships and scholarships (30,000 of them under the Expanded Programme) have been awarded since 1950.

Sometimes it is more convenient to bring these experts and groups of fellows and scholars together for instruction in new methods at training centres which may be organized for a single country, or for a group of countries facing similar development problems. The establishment of training institutes has, in fact, become one of the main instruments of the Development Decade.

The Specialized Agencies—noteworthily the ILO and UNESCO—have given such institutes a high priority in their programmes.[1]

WHAT IS A "FELLOW"?

For all the UN family, the granting of fellowships is a primary part of technical assistance, since the most important objective of technical assistance is to train people. Often this can be done in their own countries by creating schools and institutions; at other times it makes more sense to send a person abroad for a short time so that he can *see* how a problem is being handled in another country. The majority of fellowship candidates are in the administrative service of their governments or attached to some technical department. The purpose in going abroad is to learn advanced methods by observing, or taking part in, the work of an educational institution, research centre, factory, or technical establishment.

Such fellowships are frequently requested in connection with the services of UN experts. If the experts have helped to establish a school, the Government may want fellowship training for the future members of the staff. For example, two Indonesian architects were sent to take courses at Harvard and Cornell Universities in the USA, before returning to join the faculty of a School of Architecture, which a UN team had helped to organize in Bandung. Other fellows have worked as counterparts to UN experts, and then rounded out their training in other countries.

Occasionally, fellowships are given for undergraduates or graduate study leading to a degree. The situation in the newly-independent nations, where there are few people with the educational background to absorb advanced training, or where there is a serious shortage of professionals, has made such awards necessary. As a case in point, the World Health Organization has sent more than 50 young Congolese to medical schools in France and Switzerland. WHO expects to prepare 200 Congolese doctors by 1970. (There were *none* in 1960.)

The International Labour Organisation has another special arrangement, whereby it provides an opportunity for highly skilled industrial workers, foremen and other supervisors to acquire fur-

[1] See *Education and Training* (Vol. VI of *Science and Technology for Development* Series), UN, New York, 1963.

ther knowledge and skill through practical training on the shop floor in foreign industrial plants. This type of fellowship is meant to help countries which have reached a higher rung of economic and industrial development. It has been given with greater frequency in Yugoslavia than in any other country.

The average fellow goes abroad for from three to twelve months. It may be more than a year in exceptional cases, especially when a degree is involved. The fellow may be enrolled in a university course or a course at a technical institute. He may be attached, for a short while, to a research laboratory. He may be sent on an organized series of visits to government offices, factories or laboratories, scientific centres, private companies or indeed any kind of organization.

When governments request fellowship awards under the technical assistance programmes of the UN and the Agencies, they designate only the number of awards they wish, and the areas of

The United Nations Office of Public Information (OPI) launched its third Triangular Fellowship Pogramme in 1963 to assist the professional training of young journalists from Latin America, Asia and the Far East, and Africa.

study. Although a government may have, at the time of the request, a good idea of the person to whom it wants the award to go, this does not enter into the request. The grant must be approved on the basis of its importance to the economic and social development of the country, or its relevance to a particular project. The purpose of a UN fellowship is not so much to enrich the holder, as to increase his value to his country. Nevertheless, the fellow is almost always enriched by the opportunity to meet people and see situations in different lands. He comes back grateful, not just for the technical knowledge he has gained, but for the enriching personal experience he has had.

It is no coincidence that the countries which receive the most and the highest percentage of fellowships are those which have reached a more advanced stage of economic development, and have a greater pool of manpower from which to spare those who are sent abroad. A recent report by TAB shows that about 76 per cent are recorded as having introduced new techniques in their countries; over 60 per cent were engaged in teaching at the time of the inquiry; and about 80 per cent wrote, lectured, or disseminated their knowledge in some other direct way. A substantial majority (just over two-thirds) were entrusted with wider responsibilities by their Governments, after their return from abroad—which may be taken as an indication that the Governments were satisfied.

THE MEANING OF "OPEX"

On the initiative of the late Secretary-General Dag Hammarskjold, a new form of United Nations technical assistance was started in 1959, called "Opex". This scheme has taken the form of the provision of operational executive and administrative personnel (OPEX) to give high level assistance to developing countries.

Hitherto, it has been usual to send experts to *advise* a requesting government on questions of public administration. The function of such advisers has been to explain what needed to be done and how it should be done; but it remained for the Government to carry this advice into effect, with the aid of its own personnel.

A number of countries, however, have been gravely handicapped because of lack of adequately trained local personnel for carrying out the advice given by outside experts. This has been especially true of those countries which have recently attained independence, or have embarked upon big programmes of economic and social development. Such countries require the services of experts with the experience of *operating* such services. It is not sufficient to give them advice. It is necessary for outside specialists actually to perform the work themselves, until the local staff has been trained to take over.

Hence, OPEX provides for the appointment of experts at the request of governments to perform executive or administrative functions in the desired field. An OPEX expert is recruited by the technical assistance recruitment service of the United Nations and enters the service of the requesting government for the performance of such duties as may be assigned to him by that government. He is paid the same salary as a national of the country would receive had he filled the post; but the United Nations supplements this by an amount calculated to bring the expert's emoluments up to what he would have received as an advisor under the UN programmes. As stated earlier, it is an essential part of his duties to train local personnel to take his place as soon as possible.

The following typical job titles give an idea of the wide range of posts which can be covered by the OPEX programme: Air Traffic Controller; Chief Engineer; Telecommunications Manager; Director of Fisheries Operations; Chief Statistician; and Finance Officer, Ministry of Education.

When the programme started in 1959, a sum of $250,000 was allotted on the understanding that not more than 25 appointments would be made. By the end of 1961, however, eighty-one OPEX posts had been established; 26 in Asia and the Far East; 32 in Africa; 16 in Latin America and 7 in Europe and the Middle East. But since then the number of requests for this type of assistance has far exceeded the funds available. Even though the General Assembly increased the allocations in 1961 and 1962 to $850,000 for each year, there is every indication that this type of technical assistance will have to be considerably expanded. The initiative of Dag Hammarskjold has certainly been justified in the result.

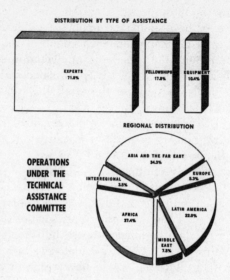

TOTAL FIELD PROGRAMME COSTS, 1961-62

DISTRIBUTION BY TYPE OF ASSISTANCE

EXPERTS
71.8%

FELLOWSHIPS
17.8%

EQUIPMENT
10.4%

REGIONAL DISTRIBUTION

OPERATIONS
UNDER THE
TECHNICAL
ASSISTANCE
COMMITTEE

ASIA AND THE FAR EAST
34.3%

EUROPE
5.3%

INTERREGIONAL
3.9%

LATIN AMERICA
22.0%

AFRICA
27.4%

MIDDLE
EAST
7.3%

A NEW VISION WANTED

To sum up, the imagination of the world has been caught by this concept of interchange of skills across frontiers and oceans. "The energies and initiative, the hopes and the capacity for self-help of many peoples have in some measure been quickened anew," runs a report of the Technical Assistance Board.

The experience of many countries has been drawn on to speed up progress where it has lagged. But, alas, it has to be admitted that, so far, the total contribution of the international programmes to the strident claims of today's economic development has been a limited one! The programmes are themselves still young; the problems which they are intended to help solve are old and vast. Operating funds are grossly inadequate and the average technical assistance project at present being undertaken is still a fairly small operation, though the Special Fund (see Chapter 6) has a larger field of operation. The aid they do provide represents only a fraction of the enormous and sustained efforts which countries in the process of development must undertake to yield enduring and worthwhile results.

One of the present handicaps is that the programmes are not directly related to any source of capital. Thus, they may help to *train* drivers for tractors or mechanics for industrial plant, but the many new opportunities opened up by such training must still depend on adequate finance from governments, private groups, or international agencies. This lack applies particularly to new ventures, which form only a part of present technical assistance programmes. The recent merger of the Special Fund and the Expanded Programme of Technical Assistance, mentioned in the final chapter of this book, is perhaps one step towards a solution.

In short, the transition from poverty and misery to a better life remains a long and arduous process. The skill-sharing programmes of the United Nations and its Specialized Agencies have begun to show what multilateral aid on a global basis *can* do for the less-developed lands. The needs of these countries far outrun the existing resources for such aid, but they do not outrun its possibilities, given a new vision of what world co-operation can mean for the achievement of the common goal.

5

How The World Bank Works

"Any country or group of countries prepared to adopt eco-
omic development as a central objective of its policy will find the
Bank, together with its affiliates, a willing and, I hope, a powerful ally", declared Mr. George D. Woods, President of the World
Bank, speaking to the 120 national representatives assembled at
the Geneva World Trade Conference in March 1964. He was
describing the Bank's increasing role in helping needy countries
onto their financial feet. And that is the subject of this chapter.

The World Bank is one of the foundation-stones of the new
international economic order which the World Trade Conference
could clearly discern arising on the crumbling remnants of Adam
Smith's vanished dream of an automatically-adjusting system of
self-sufficient nations. At the risk of some overlapping, we must
turn back in this chapter to the beginnings of the World Bank.
At the same time, a brief description must be given of the two
affiliated bodies of the Bank, namely, the International Finance
Corporation (IFC) and the International Development Association (IDA). A sister United Nations Specialized Agency, the International Monetary Fund (IMF), will also have a place in our
survey, since it co-operates closely with the Bank.

If the present chapter deals mainly with organizational questions, it is because, without such an administrative framework,
the more spectacular achievements listed in our other chapters
would lack that unity and stability which are essential to orderly
progress in economic development.

TWENTY YEARS OF BUILDING

The World Bank was founded during the last stages of the
Second World War, at an economic conference of the wartime

allies held at Bretton Woods in July 1944. It began operations in June 1946. Its first loans were made in 1947 to countries in dire need of rebuilding their shattered economies. A total of $500 million was, in fact, lent by the Bank for immediate European postwar reconstruction.

Since 1948, more and more of its funds have been directed to the less-developed areas of the world. By the end of 1963, the Bank had made 371 loans, totalling nearly $7,630 million. This immense sum has been used to finance more than 800 projects in 70 countries.

At the present time, the distribution of Bank lending, divided between the main regions of the world, is as follows: Africa $1,002 million; Asia and Middle East $2,643 million; Australia $418 million; New Zealand $40 million; Europe $1,713 million; and the Western Hemisphere $2,050 million. What these global figures mean in terms of actual physical and social progress on the ground level can best be seen in studying some of the specific projects given later on.

In a nutshell, the purpose of the Bank is to make loans where private capital is not available on reasonable terms to member countries who need to finance productive enterprises. The Bank also provides a wide range of technical assistance to its members. It may lend to member governments, governmental agencies, and even to private enterprises; but if the borrower is not a government, the guarantee of the member government is required for the loan.

HOW THE BANK IS RUN

The Bank's membership now consists of the governments of 102 countries. Each member subscribes to the Bank's capital stock in relation to its economic strength and nominates a Governor to the Bank's Board of Governors. The Board meets once a year; but it has delegated most of its powers to 20 Executive Directors —five Directors, who represent the five largest stockholders, and 15 Directors elected by the other member countries.

The Executive Directors are responsible for matters of policy and meet at least once each month. They have to approve all proposals for loans. But the day-to-day conduct of the Bank's operations is the responsibility of its President, who is also Chairman of the Executive Directors.

The Bank has a total staff of over 900 persons, who represent more than 60 nationalities and include bankers, economists, accountants, engineers, and other experts. Resident advisers are from time to time stationed in the countries who so request, and the Bank has recently established a career service of such advisers. The headquarters of the Bank are in Washington, D.C., while branch offices exist in Paris and New York.

SOME OVERALL FIGURES

A few round figures will help to give a general picture of the size of the Bank's operations. (A more detailed list of the Bank's transactions is given in the free literature, mailed on request.) Like ordinary national banks, the World Bank is both a lender and a borrower. But, theoretically, it operates on the capital subscribed by its member governments. By May 1964, the total of this subscribed capital was just over $21,000 million. Of this amount, however, only the equivalent of about $2,000 million had been paid in, partly in gold or dollars and partly in local currencies. The remainder is subject to call if required to meet the Bank's obligations, in accordance with normal practice in banking circles.

Whereas, the Bank has already paid out nearly $6,000 million on its loans, it has financed less than one-third of this from its subscriptions. The remainder of its funds comes mainly from the sale of its bonds in the world's capital markets. By April 1964, the Bank had outstanding borrowings of about $2,500 million, mostly in the form of U.S. dollar bonds; but over half of these are owed to investors *outside* the United States.

Private investors have bought some of its loans, and thus the Bank has added another $1,763 million to the funds already available for the kind of development financing described below. The rate of interest charged by the Bank is based on the rate which it would itself have to pay to borrow money at the time the loan is made (plus a 1 per cent annual commission charge and a small additional fraction for administration costs). The long-term lending rate of the Bank in the past five years has been roughly between 5½ and 6 per cent.

LOANS FOR GROWTH

Where do the loans go?

They go primarily to helping member countries to strengthen their economic foundations and so ensure their future prosperity. This is called broadly "development lending", and is far removed from any "give-away" policy. Approximately one-third of it has been devoted directly to the provision of electric power: it has helped to add over 20 million kilowatts to the world's generating capacity. Another third has gone to basic transport—railways, highways, air and water-ways. The remaining third has been allocated both to agriculture, especially for irrigation, and for industry, especially for steel production.

Communications are being improved and workshops modernized in Nigeria, where the Development Program is being carried out with the help of several loans from the World Bank. Two Hausa women walk by the new Dindima Bridge.

Three simple principles govern these lending operations. First, the borrower must be in a position to repay the loan. Second, the project to be financed must be of such benefit to the economy as to justify the borrowing economically. Third, the project must be well planned and feasible of execution.

Before making a loan, the Bank satisfies itself that the borrower —whether a government, autonomous agency, or private corporation—will be able to service the debt. The Bank then investigates the project in detail, the economic and financial returns expected, and the kind of management proposed. Only when this examination is completed, is the loan negotiated.

One further point should be noted. The Bank never lends the total cost of a project. It normally finances only the *foreign exchange costs* involved in the purchase of goods and services which have to be imported into the country to carry out the project. Local costs—which often come to more than half of the total —have to be met by the borrower out of other resources. Although all orders for goods and services are placed by the borrowers, the Bank insists on the use of efficient methods and it usually requires international competition in placing such orders.

Finally, while the project is being carried through, it is inspected by members of the Bank staff, and the borrower is required to make regular progress reports. Moreover, the Bank keeps in touch with the completed project throughout the life of the loan.

So much for the elementary mechanics of loan-making by the World Bank.

SOME CONCRETE RESULTS

As indicated above, most of the Bank's development loans have been for basic utilities, such as electric power ($2,710 million), transportation ($2,519 million), industry ($1,165 million) and agriculture ($560 million).

Why should two-thirds of the Bank's lending have been thus devoted to power and transport? The answer is that adequate power and transport facilities are vital to modern economic progress. Right from 1948, therefore, the Bank has been helping to build these foundations of economic development in the less-developed countries. On such a basis alone can the expansion of industrial and agricultural activities be assured.

The above simple statistics do not tell the full story of the impact of the Bank's assistance on the lot of the ordinary people in the less-developed world. Thousands of jobs have been created in new or expanded industries in the towns. Farmers have been able to increase their yields, market more efficiently their produce, and earn a decent living. Electricity and modern irrigation facilities have been introduced in many districts which never knew them before. For the first time, isolated areas have been opened up for cultivation or commercial activity.

Examples from three different countries will help to explain what this initiative means in local terms.

In Ecuador, the Bank financed the construction of a new highway network, which opened up fertile lands that had previously been covered with jungle. Along the new roads, settlers came to work in this hot coastal plain, which had never been cultivated before. Soon the jungle was converted into one of the world's largest banana-producing areas and Ecuador became a large exporter of bananas. But economic growth is never an isolated event. The banana development imposed heavy strains on Ecuador's only port, the river port of Guayaquil. Thus, port development followed and helped further to stimulate Ecuador's commerce and employment.

In 1953, the old Pacifico Railroad of Mexico had remained in a dilapidated condition for nearly 70 years. The right-of-way was overgrown; there was practically no ballast; and 40 per cent of the ties required immediate replacement. Frequent train derailments had brought traffic speeds down to six miles an hour. This was at a time when the expanding Mexican economy most needed an efficient railroad system, especially to carry away the harvests of its rapidly-developing Northwest region. By 1957, however, the completion of the railroad rehabilitation programme had brought about a dramatic change—as the result of a $61 million World Bank loan. Copper mined in Cananea, near the United States border, could now make its journey to Guadalajara in eight days, compared with 50 days previously. Agricultural produce, which took almost the same time for the journey in 1952,

71

When completed this Hydro-Electric Development Project in Brazil, assisted by World Bank loans, will supply power to major electric utilities operating in a region in which four-fifths of the country's industries and much of the agricultural activity is concentrated.

now takes about three days, and it also has ready access to profitable markets all over the United States.

The Dez River Project, in the Khuzistan Province of Iran was inaugurated by the Shah in 1963. South-western Iran was once the fertile granary of the Persian Empire, but it had become a pale shadow of its former fruitfulness. As a first step toward helping Khuzistan to regain its ancient position, a high dam has been constructed on the Dez River to irrigate 360,000 acres of land, produce electric power, and control the floods. The Bank backed this undertaking with a loan of $42 million. So today, the 620-foot high dam stands as a symbol of new hope to the people of Khuzistan and a monument to international economic co-operation.

NOT BY MONEY ALONE

The Bank realized quite early that loans alone could not ensure rapid economic progress. They must be supplemented by technical assistance on a wide scale. In most less-developed countries, inexperience and the lack of trained manpower at every level are as serious a handicap as lack of capital. Hence, the technical assistance services of the Bank Group have become increasingly valuable over the years. Some practical examples will make this clear.

Today, most developing countries have development plans in operation. But things were different in 1949, when the Bank first began to assist less-developed countries to plan long-term programmes. At that time, requests for loans were hardly more than lists of ideas for projects which the Government had under consideration. They contained little detailed engineering preparation, and even less data on the priorities of the proposed projects or their place in the economic pattern of the country as a whole. Then, again, missions sent by the Bank noted the absence of effective government machinery charged with designing an overall framework of development.

As a beginning in 1949, the Bank, at the request of the Government of Colombia, organized a survey mission to analyze the Colombian economy and to make recommendations for a long-term programme. The results of this initiative convinced the Bank that this type of assistance was indispensable. By 1963, Bank survey mission reports had been prepared on more than twenty countries: Colombia, Turkey, Nicaragua, Guatemala, Cuba, Iraq, Ceylon, Surinam, Jamaica, British Guiana, Nigeria, Malaya, Syria, Jordan, Italian Somaliland, Thailand, Libya, Tanganyika, Venezuela, Uganda, Spain and Kenya.

The object of these preliminary missions is to estimate the amount of investment which a country *can* undertake with the resources at its command; to recommend priorities for public investment, after taking private investment requirements into account; and to suggest economic and financial policies to assure the success of the programme. In several cases, the Bank has also provided consultants to help member governments to put their mission recommendations into effect.

ALLIES OF PROGRESS

In providing assistance to the developing countries, the Bank has received the cooperation of many other organizations, as we noted in chapter 2. For example, FAO has nominated agricultural experts for the survey missions. WHO has helped to recruit public health experts, and UNESCO has sent educational experts. Experts have also been loaned by various member governments. It is not only the advanced nations who are thus contributing their trained personnel; the developing nations as well are helping each other. More than one-fifth of the international experts now conducting technical assistance projects for ILO in Africa, Asia and Latin America come from underdeveloped countries.

In recent years, requests from member governments for resident advisers to assist them on problems of economic development have outstripped the amount of help the Bank can provide from its own staff. Accordingly, in 1962, the Bank set up a Development Advisory Service, offering a full-time career to qualified experts to assist governments on their own major policy problems. Some of these experts are now working in Colombia, Ghana, Honduras, Libya, Pakistan and Thailand.

In 1956, the Bank established the Economic Development Institute (EDI) to serve as a "staff college" for senior officials from less-developed countries working on development projects. The Bank has donated through EDI economic development libraries to central banks, finance ministries, and planning bodies in the less-developed countries, first in English, then in French.

"One of the most critical elements in the economic progress of the underdeveloped countries," states the Bank's current Annual Report, "continues to be the skill brought not only to development programming, but to the management of economic affairs in general. The Bank's chief instrument for fostering this skill is the Economic Development Institute. . . . In the past year, the Institute greatly expanded its work, providing courses in more subjects, to more students, and in more languages, than ever before. One example is the course on project evaluation inaugurated during the year. This course, given in English, was introduced to help increase the capacity of member countries to appraise and prepare development projects, so as to make efficient use of domestic financial resources and development assistance from abroad."

Not least, the Bank has worked closely with the International Development Association (IDA), which was set up in 1960 as an affiliate of the Bank. The Association shares the same management and staff with the Bank. IDA's main purpose is to help to meet the situation of that growing number of countries who need outside capital, but who are not able to service *ordinary* loans. Hence, IDA extends credits on easier terms than the burden of servicing a Bank loan. Up to May 1964, IDA has extended credits of $612 million to 51 member countries. These credits have been made payable over fifty years, and are free of interest, carrying only a small service charge.

Under an IDA credit, for instance, equivalent to $1.5 million, which was extended to Niger in June 1964, a 21-mile earth road from Damthiao to Dungass will be improved and a new road of about the same length will be built from Dungass to Maigatari on the Niger-Nigerian border, to facilitate the transport of groundnuts, the chief export, for shipment overseas via the Nigerian transport system. This credit is for a term of 50 years; repayment of principal will not begin until January 1975, after a 10-year period of grace. There will be no interest, but a service charge of three-quarters of 1 per cent will be made to cover IDA's administrative costs.

The Association has given special attention to the problems of education—its planning, administration and financing. Thus, IDA has been able to help countries to understand better the methods for planning their educational investments; and especially to provide architectural and other assistance to ensure that best value is obtained from the money spent on school buildings. A recent example of this kind of assistance is given at the end of this chapter.

The adaptability of IDA is shown by the fact that at the 1964 Geneva Trade Conference the proposed scheme for "compensatory financing," which many countries have requested (due to their lack of foreign exchange), would probably be administered by the International Development Association, but only after the country concerned had had recourse to the short-term compensatory financing facilities supplied by the International Monetary Fund (described below). Such compensatory financing would be regarded as "supplementary and complementary" to the normal commodity arrangements, but it would involve gaining new resources for IDA.

"In my view," says Paul G. Hoffman, "at least half of the $14 billion in additional investment in the underdeveloped countries during the Development Decade should be channeled through the International Development Association, the new UN enterprise associated with the World Bank. This international lending agency is off to a good start, but its rate of lending—at $200 million a year—is well below the amount needed. IDA specializes in fifty-year interest-free loans for just the kind of projects we have been discussing. There is an urgent need for it to expand its operations rapidly, and I cannot see how the need for the IDA-type of loan can be met with anything less than $1 billion of investment per year."[1]

"VENTURE" CAPITAL AND SAFETY VALVES

Then, there is a further affiliate, the International Finance Corporation (IFC), which plays a different role in the production process. In addition to the Bank's normal lending for large private industrial corporations in less-developed countries, private industry often requires finance in the form of what is called "equity participation," that is, sharing the risks of the enterprise. To help with these problems, the Bank established the IFC in 1956. Membership is open to all governments which are members of the Bank. The President of the Bank is also the President of IFC and the Executive Directors of the Bank, appointed or elected by member governments, serve also as Directors of IFC.

IFC has an authorized capital of $110 million, of which $99 million has been subscribed by seventy-eight member governments. By April 1964, it had made seventy-three investments for a total of $100.9 million, located in 27 countries of Asia, Africa, Latin America, the Middle East and Australia. The industries mainly involved covered rubber products, cement, cotton textiles, electrical equipment, and automobile parts.

The main purpose of IFC is, therefore, to stimulate the growth of industry in the developing countries by investing without government guarantees in *private* enterprises. Thus, the Bank and IFC perform a complementary role: the first provides long-term fixed interest loans and the second supplies "venture" capital.

Industrialization, it need hardly be said, is one of the essential stages in economic development. Successful industrialization de-

[1] Paul G. Hoffman: *World Without Want*, Harper & Row, New York, 1962.

76

pends on modern manufacturing techniques, competent management, technicians and other skilled personnel, and, of course, capital. Some of these can be imported, as they often have been in the past; but only a few relatively large-scale industries in developing countries can hope to obtain foreign capital and management directly.

Small and medium-sized industries must usually depend on local resources of skill and finance. Hence, to increase the supply of these ingredients, many countries have established special institutions to mobilize their own resources of capital and know-how. These are generally known as "development banks." Consequently, the World Bank and IFC have together helped to set up a type of development bank more usually called industrial development finance companies.

Without going into a more technical discussion, Morocco can be given as an example of this joint action. The Moroccan Development Bank, started by the Government in 1956, received a $15 million foreign exchange loan from the World Bank and an "equity" investment of $1.5 million from the IFC.

In this connexion, attention should be drawn to the important functions of a parallel agency of the United Nations, which is one of the Bank's allies—the oldest, in fact—namely, the International Monetary Fund (IMF). The Fund came into existence in December 1945 and acts as a system of cash reserves that member nations can draw upon to meet temporary deficits in their international trade. Nations that join the Bank must, in fact, first be members of the Fund. Each member is assigned a "quota" in the Fund and its subscription is usually equal to its quota.

The Fund has to try to solve some knotty problems at times, but one such example must suffice at this point. When a country buys more from abroad than it sells abroad, it has to find foreign currency ("foreign exchange") to pay the deficit. Such payments are generally drawn from the country's reserves of gold or of foreign money in pounds or dollars. But if these reserves become exhausted, the country concerned may be driven to set up trade barriers or resort to other restrictive devices which will only, in the end, injure world trade.

One purpose of the Fund, therefore, is to act as a kind of safety valve, that is to say, to provide a reserve of foreign exchange so

77

as to make possible an easing of the member's trade position. The Directors have wide powers to restrict or expand the amount of help they decide to give to a member, according to whether the member is, in their opinion, taking the correct action to balance its trade in the long run.

COOPERATION ON THE TOP LEVEL

Coordination between the Bank and the United Nations in technical assistance and in other fields has been made clear in earlier chapters, and further illustrations of this will follow in due course. It is effected by a Liaison Committee composed of the UN Secretary-General, the Managing-Director of the Special Fund, the Executive Chairman of the Technical Assistance Board, and the President of the Bank and IDA. Members of the Liaison Committee consult with each other on current programmes and common plans.

A particularly close relationship exists between the Bank and the United Nations Special Fund, one of whose primary purposes is to arrange "pre-investment" studies in less-developed countries. This special task will be explained in Chapter 6. Such studies are often intricate and costly; but they are essential preparations for the financing of major projects by the Bank, since the Bank can only invest its capital, as we noted, after a careful appraisal has been made of the success of the loan.

One example can be seen in the survey for the Niger Dam in Nigeria, in order to ascertain the merits of constructing a dam for electric power generation, navigation, flood control and irrigation. Other recent studies have concerned telecommunication needs in Central America, power requirements in the Sudan, and coal resources in Colombia.

In stressing cooperation, however, it should never be forgotten that it is the *independence* of the Bank, as a world institution, which does so much to enhance its value to the countries it assists. This point was expressed by the Bank's President (Mr. George D. Woods) at a meeting of the United Nations Economic and Social Council in 1963, in the following terms:

> "Because the World Bank has no political or commercial axe to grind, its officers can speak completely frankly. We can point out the advantages or disadvantages of a course of

action. We can state the position of the Bank in any matter in dispute, without being suspected of bias. We can act as 'honest broker' when difficulties arise. From the point of view of a member country, we represent an institution which need not be regarded either as patron or supplicant. From this position, it is possible to discuss and sometimes resolve problems that for reasons of mutual distrust or national dignity might well have been insoluble in the framework of negotiations between individual governments."

THE SEARCH FOR MINERALS

This chapter can best be concluded by selecting two somewhat diverse activities illustrating how wide is the Bank's span of operations—in this case, stretching from minerals to education.

Many World Bank loans have been made to areas in which mineral development plays a leading role in the national economy. For example: $16 million was loaned to Australia in 1956 to import mining equipment; $40 million to the Congo in 1957 for road building; and $50 million to Algeria in 1959 to finance a petroleum pipeline. But recent loans to Gabon and Mauritania are instructive because they belong to a different category. In both these cases the Bank helped to finance a new mineral development in an underdeveloped country where the material cannot at present be used locally, but where the production itself would prove an asset in developing the economy of the country.

In June 1959, the Bank made a $35 million loan for the extraction of manganese deposits in the Gabon Republic, for the financing of equipment and services for mining operations, for the construction of a 45-mile cableway, and for the building of an 180-mile railway to transport the ore to the Atlantic Ocean. The project was aimed at an initial production of 500,000 tons annually. The ore is high-grade, and conditions were favourable to open-pit operations; but the development of the mine itself is only a small part of the total investment. The project also covers living quarters, workshops, electric power, and other facilities at the side of the mine, as well as transportation, storage and loading facilities. All this will be bound to have important side effects in opening up large new areas in both Gabon and the Republic of the Congo to other forms of economic activity as production increases.

Similarly, in March 1960, the World Bank made a loan of $66 million for the development of iron ore in Mauritania in northwest Africa. About twice the size of France, Mauritania is populated by less than a million people, most of whom are nomads. About 90 per cent of the workers live from subsistence agriculture. Wage and salary earners are largely employed by the Government. Yet the key to Mauritania's future development would appear to lie in its mineral resources, particularly in the rich iron ore deposit. In comparison with the present economy, the project is indeed immense. The investment is, in fact, six times the size of the current national income and it is estimated that the potential value of the iron ore will be at least five times as great as all present exports from Mauritania.

"Something of the philosophy of the World Bank of financing mineral development can be learned from these two loans," states Professor James F. McDivitt, of Pennsylvania State University: "Both are in somewhat isolated countries of low population, with relatively poor financial resources. . . . It is in areas such as these that mineral development is of particular importance and provides perhaps the greatest hope for the future."[2]

EDUCATION IS WEALTH

Only in recent years have educationists begun to think in terms of economics. Previously, most stress has been laid on the *right* of people to receive the benefits of education. But recently it has become the practice to envisage education as a development of *human resources*—that is to say, to regard popular education as an organic part of the total social and economic wealth of a country.

Pakistan provides our final example. In March 1964, IDA extended two credits, totalling $13 million, to Pakistan for educational projects. These credits will cover half the cost of improving agricultural and technical education, including the establishment of two agricultural universities, 14 technical institutes and three teacher training colleges. The increase in trained personnel for agriculture and industry, made possible by this expansion, will reduce the critical shortage of manpower which is at present hampering the economic growth of Pakistan. The low productiv-

---

[2] See *Journal of Metals*, New York, July 1963.

ity of agriculture throughout the country points to a need for trained personnel for research, training, and extension services. Agriculture accounts for three-quarters of total employment in Pakistan, yet only 2 per cent of students enrolled in higher education are specializing in agriculture. Thanks to the credits, however, the new agricultural training programme aims at an annual output of 570 agricultural graduates by 1965, and 840 by 1970 —compared with about 200 in 1960.

Similarly, a shortage of technical skills among the labour force in Pakistan is one of the reasons why output per man in industry has failed to increase in recent years. About 850 industrial technicians were trained in 1962, but the estimated requirement for 1970 is 7,000. It is believed that the IDA credits will contribute at least 1,700 of this number. The credits given to technical institutes will also be used to install equipment for classrooms, laboratories, libraries, workshops, student hostels, and administrative offices; while the aid to teacher-training colleges will make possible an expansion of training programmes in specialized fields. Altogether, the educational improvement plan in Pakistan, made possible by these credits, is estimated to cost $26 million, and it will be due for completion in 1968.

Thus, another realistic target has been set up by the financial agencies of international cooperation and another venture in the development of a nation's human resources has been well begun.

6

"Seed Money" And The Special Fund

The ever-expanding programme of United Nations assistance entered a new and promising phase on the 1st of January, 1959, with the inauguration of the Special Fund. The Special Fund is not itself a source of new capital, as its title might imply; but it makes the investment of capital feasible and profitable, by laying down the groundwork for the sound investment of "capital," in the broad sense in which it is used in this chapter. Hence, the Special Fund is generally identified with the somewhat vague term "pre-investment," which will require examination in the course of the following pages.

The Special Fund carries the technical assistance programmes, previously described, a big step forward by helping the developing countries to lay a firm foundation for their major developments in practically every field. It is designed to assist these countries *to develop their national wealth through their own resources.* So it carries the concept of "capital investment" far beyond the usual notion of financial aid expressed in terms of external money grants or loans.

One way in which it does this is by financing surveys, so as to obtain the *basic information* about a country's wealth-producing resources, without which the planners would work in the dark. Research institutes are set up with assistance from the Fund to study the sources and uses of local materials; and training institutes are likewise set up to develop technicians, craftsmen, and experts with specialized skills.

The overall objectives of the Fund may therefore be summarized as follows:

    (1) to help the developing countries to discover and utilize their natural sources;

    (2) to organise educational and technical training programmes, so as to bring out the full potentialities of their skilled manpower;

    (3) to promote sound development planning; and

    (4) to assist applied research organizations, so as to use modern scientific methods to speed up industrial and other development.

"Searching for investment opportunity," says Paul G. Hoffman, Managing-Director of the Special Fund, in his *World Without Want*, "is known as 'pre-investment' work. Its value has been proven time and time again. The United Nations Special Fund went into Argentina in 1959 and 1960 to find out where electric power was most needed, and where it could be produced. The survey cost the United Nations $300,000. Spending only that much, British and American engineers and economists found ways in which no less than $735 million could be profitably invested over a ten-year period to provide urgently needed electricity for Argentine industry and homes."[1]

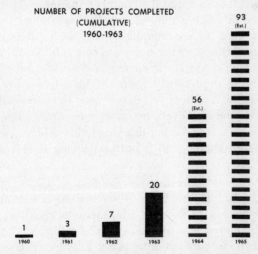

NUMBER OF PROJECTS COMPLETED
(CUMULATIVE)
1960-1963

[1] Paul G. Hoffman: *World Without Want*, Harper and Row, New York, 1962.

83

The example which Mr. Hoffman cites well illustrates how a relatively modest expenditure by the Special Fund can dramatically improve a country's production potential. The Argentine programme aims at meeting power needs in six important regions of the country, through construction of seventeen thermal-electric and four hydro-electric projects and the extension of distribution networks. Although this pre-investment survey cost the Special Fund only $300,000, as stated above, it has already brought forth over $300 *million* of finance towards the recommended $735 million ten-year investment programme. This search for "investment opportunity" has clearly been justified by the results.

SMALL FISH BRING BIG RETURNS

How the Fund operates can best be shown by actual examples of projects undertaken, such as the foregoing. This chapter will select a number of others from the growing portfolio of the Fund's achievements. Nor will it escape observation how much has been achieved in so short a period since the Fund was established.

Peru is a further case in point. The Peruvian Government requested the Special Fund in 1959 for assistance in setting up a research institute to study the country's marine resources and to develop new fishing techniques, as well as to examine the economics of marketing. As a consequence, the Marine Resources Institute was established and it has since concentrated on anchovies. The "anchoveta" is caught in enormous quantities and turned into fishmeal for feeding farm livestock. This harvest from the sea now forms the backbone of Peru's new industry—although, in another way, the anchoveta has always been a source of wealth to Peru, for on this and other fish feed millions of seabirds, whose droppings form *guano*, a rich fertilizer which Peru has exported for many years.

Another type of operation can be seen in Ghana, where the great flood plain of the Volta River had been virtually lost to human use because of flooding. The survey of the flood plain was recently completed with the active collaboration of FAO. It has shown that the installation of irrigation and drainage systems can provide highly suitable conditions for the growing of rice and sugar cane, as well as groundnuts, maise, and animal fodder. In

84

the course of the survey, detailed studies were made of the topography and soil. It calls for the development of eight pilot areas encompassing about 21,000 acres of land suitable for cultivation.

Using this information, development schemes were prepared for the pilot areas. By allotting 11,000 acres for rice-growing, it is estimated that the yield will be about 2 million pounds of unhusked rice per year. Two thousand acres to be used for other crops, such as maize, groundnuts, and animal fodders, are expected to go a long way towards meeting domestic needs for these products. The 8,000 acres earmarked for the growing of sugar cane are already regarded as the basis of a new sugar industry.

These schemes call for a long-term investment of approximately $14 million in irrigation and drainage systems and the building of new settlements. But it promises a rich reward. For example, the production of sugar and rice and other crops would sharply reduce the need for imports of these foodstuffs and probably result in a saving in foreign exchange for Ghana of nearly $5 million a year. On the strength of this survey, the Government has awarded a $3 million contract to an engineering firm to construct the irrigation works. At the same time, an offer of a long-term credit loan ($14 million) has been made by the Polish Government to establish a sugar factory.

MEANING OF "PRE-INVESTMENT"

By making possible projects such as these, the Fund acts as a bridge between the technical assistance experts, who can give good advice, and the actual investment of new capital that must come later. The Fund has thus been concentrating on "pre-investment" programmes of this order.

"The emphasis on pre-investment activity is one of the really useful developments of recent years," says a British observer of Special Fund activities across the world: "The idea is that people should be encouraged to spend more money in preparing the ground before they import a lot of capital for a project—for instance, in measuring as precisely as possible the return that they are likely to get from this project, compared with other alternatives; in training local technicians and managers who will be capable of operating it; and in studying the implications of the

85

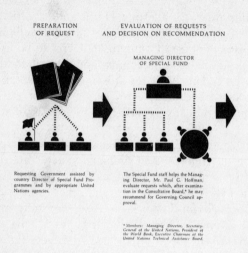

PREPARATION
OF REQUEST

EVALUATION OF REQUESTS
AND DECISION ON RECOMMENDATION

MANAGING DIRECTOR
OF SPECIAL FUND

Requesting Government assisted by country Director of Special Fund Programmes and by appropriate United Nations agencies.

The Special Fund staff helps the Managing Director, Mr. Paul G. Hoffman, evaluate requests which, after examination in the Consultative Board,* he may recommend for Governing Council approval.

*Members: Managing Director, Secretary-General of the United Nations, President of the World Bank, Executive Chairman of the United Nations Technical Assistance Board.

STEPS TO

project in terms of the demand that it will make on other economic resources. . . . It takes up to five years to establish the basic facts about the flow of a river, which must be known before it is possible to begin to work out a comprehensive scheme for power and irrigation."[2]

The Fund's main functions can thus be seen to fall into three major categories. In the first place come projects concerned with *natural resources*. These usually take the form of surveys, for example, of mineral deposits, forest resources, or possibilities for hydro-power or for land utilization, as in Ghana. Similarly, "feasibility studies," as they are termed, are set on foot for transportation or communication networks, which are so essential to the industrial development of a country.

[2] Andrew Shonfield: *The Attack on World Poverty,* Vintage Book, New York, 1962.

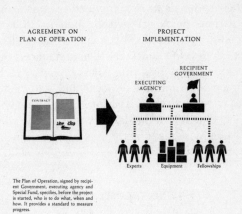

RECIPIENT
GOVERNMENT

EXECUTING
AGENCY

Experts   Equipment   Fellowships

The Plan of Operation, signed by recipient Government, executing agency and Special Fund, specifies, before the project is started, who is to do what, when and how. It provides a standard to measure progress.

ACHIEVEMENT

Next come *research facilities for economic development,* such as that already described in the case of Peru. Projects in this group usually comprise the setting up of applied research institutes to define industrial potentials, promote better use of local materials, improve manufacturing techniques, design new equipment, and carry out studies to raise productivity.

The third category contains projects aimed at the development of the *human resources* of the developing countries. These consist of training projects within the countries concerned and they are usually on a larger scale than is possible under the United Nations training programmes mentioned earlier. Perhaps the most significant part of the Special Fund programme, in fact, is concerned with helping developing countries to build up a labour force suitable for industrial expansion. Hence, a large part of Special Fund assistance to industry has been devoted to training technical instructors, managers, supervisors, and foremen, so that they can pass on their knowledge and skills to industrial workers.

"By the end of 1963," said Mr. Paul G. Hoffman at the twelfth session of the Fund's Governing Council in June 1964, "approximately 45,000 nationals have completed or are taking advanced courses in various fields of specialization in 78 Special Fund-assisted training institutions. This achievement will have a 'multiplier effect' on development." He then announced that of the 23 surveys of natural resources thus far completed, 12 had already generated over $600 million of local and external investment. "The impact of Special Fund assistance," the Managing-Director continued, "is being felt in the daily lives of people who are eating more food, using more manufactured products, enjoying improved public services, and finding increased employment with rising income."

FINDING THE "SEED" MONEY

It should be noted that the Special Fund does not itself carry out the projects which it assists. It has, so far, made arrangements with the United Nations and its Specialized Agencies to undertake the projects in question. Thus, they become the executing agencies for the Fund. An essential feature of the Fund's projects is that they should show important results in a comparatively short time. In the case of the institutes, the country should be in a position to take them over when the period of assistance has elapsed.

The overall growth of these operations in so brief a period is significant. By the end of 1960, the Special Fund had approved 115 projects calling for total expenditures of $225 million. The Fund contributed $96 million of this amount, an average of $834,000 per project. The developing countries receiving this assistance themselves contributed $129 million for their projects —the major share of total costs.

By the end of 1963, the Fund had provided $250 million for 286 projects, financed mainly by the voluntary pledges of 102 Governments. These 286 major development projects were carried out in 96 low-income countries and territories. Of these, 118 projects are intensive studies of natural resources and productive capacity in 63 under-developed countries and territories, and 168

The University of Engineering and Technology in Lahore, Pakistan, is being assisted by the United Nations Special Fund in carrying out its programme to increase the number of engineers and other technical personnel.

are concerned with training, education and research in 83 low-income countries. The latter prepare administrators, engineers, teachers, technicians, marketing specialists and economic planners, all of whom are needed to make better use of the countries' resources.

The present programme of 421 projects costs $919 million. The counterpart contribution of the recipient governments came to the equivalent of $545 million, while the Special Fund contribution was $374 million. It will thus be seen that *more than half* of the cost is met from the assisted countries themselves. Yet, without the Fund's "seed money", the balance could never have been so profitably used.

It is encouraging to realise that the Governments of low-income and high-income countries alike have been steadily increasing their voluntary contributions to the Special Fund. Pledges totalled $26 million for 1959. They rose to $39 million for 1960, to $48 million in 1961, and to $60 million in 1962. For 1963, they amounted to $73 million. Special Fund "seed money" vitally needed for 1965 to carry out essential activities was estimated by Mr. Hoffman (June 1964) at $200 million. By 1970, he added, "the needs of developing countries for our technical and pre-investment assistance will require double that amount."

ON THE JOB

Thus far, at least 1,840 experts from 64 countries have used their specialized skills on difficult and challenging assignments in 260 separate projects in over 100 countries and territories. More are on the way; and these include administrators, agronomists, architects, cartographers, economists, engineers, foresters, geologists, planners, researchers, statisticians, surveyors, teachers, and veterinarians.

Over seventy field officers help the governments and the United Nations agencies to carry out the projects. Their directors advise on the preparation of applications for Special Fund assistance. These field officers are at the constant disposal of the recipient countries who are seeking assistance, so as to render their aid more effective.

The way these services operate can best be understood by looking at further examples from three different parts of the world.

In Nigeria, a dam site survey of the Niger River, completed by the World Bank as executing agency for the Special Fund in 1961, recommended the construction of a hydro-electric dam at Kainji. The Bank has agreed to assist the Government of Nigeria by making a loan equivalent to $82 million as part of a $208 million investment required for the initial phase. Completion of this phase will meet Nigerian electricity requirements for the next thirty years. The dam would open the Niger River to commercial navigation from its mouth right up to communities in the neighbouring Republic of Niger. It also offers flood control for hundreds of miles downstream, enabling much land to be brought into production. Not least, it will provide something like an annual catch of 10,000 tons of fish from the 100-mile long lake behind the dam.

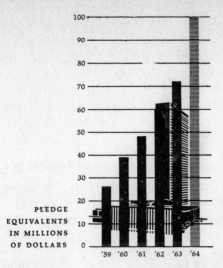

PLEDGE
EQUIVALENTS
IN MILLIONS
OF DOLLARS

In the Republic of China, water development plans have been formulated by the Government as a result of a Special Fund assisted survey completed by the United Nations. Further Special Fund assistance is directed to studies of the Choshui and Wu River basins, to improve existing irrigation works, to ascertain hydro-power capacity, and to examine ways of controlling the flood waters. Meanwhile, 302 wells have been drilled and equipped with pumps during the project period, and the Government has received a loan of $3.7 million from the International Development Association for drilling a further 765 wells.

In Thailand, a survey of the Nam Pong River has recently been completed. It recommends a multipurpose water-resource development plan which includes the construction of a dam, power-plant and distribution system, and irrigation canals. The Thailand Government has lost no time to find ways to finance the construction and has concluded an agreement with the Federal Republic of Germany for $11 million of the $17 million needed, the remaining $6 million coming from Thai sources.

In Laos, a similar survey of the Nam Ngum River has recommended the construction of a storage dam and related irrigation and drainage works. The benefits which could be derived from this relatively small scheme are cheaper electricity, which would remove a serious obstacle to the development and expansion of local industry, and irrigation and flood control, which would per-

91

mit double-cropping. The annual income per hectare of agricultural land will then increase enormously and the country's dependence on imported staple foods be greatly reduced, at the same time providing steady employment for many thousands of people. In comparison with such wide benefits, the estimated cost is by no means large: namely, $22 million of external finance for the entire scheme. The Government of Laos is at present actively seeking this capital.

THE MEANING OF HUMAN RESOURCES

So far, we have dealt mainly with developing natural resources. But human resources are even more vital. Since all economic development depends on the very people whose well-being it seeks to ensure, the Special Fund attaches great importance to this human "potential." All projects that it assists contain elements of training, including fellowships for foreign study; but over 40 per cent of the Special Fund's resources is now being devoted to projects having technical education and training as their main objective.

By mid-March, 1963, 74 education and training programmes were functioning. Under these, some 3,500 engineering students were enrolled in universities and about 4,350 more were attending polytechnic institutes. In additon, Special Fund industrial training centres were upgrading the skills of some 7,500 teachers, foremen, and supervisors; and nearly 4,600 had already completed their training under these programmes. For instance, over 600 trainees were taking courses in civil aviation schools, while 600 had graduated from them. A few recent examples of this type of activity must again suffice. They illustrate, particularly, how the Fund co-operates with the other United Nations agencies.

The acute shortage of trained personnel in many developing countries demonstrates the fundamental importance of training. Hence, the main objective of nearly a dozen Special Fund-assisted projects is to strengthen agricultural institutions. One such institution is located in Liberia. Although 80 per cent of that country's population is engaged in subsistence agriculture, training facilities in agricultural extension work did not exist until the Government obtained Special Fund/FAO assistance in 1961 for the setting up of a College of Agriculture in Monrovia. The

College is now offering a four-year degree course in which thirty students are currently enrolled.

In Colombia, a Special Fund programme is training instructors for the National Apprenticeship Service, under the control of ILO. Courses are being given in automobile, diesel and other mechanics, electric trades, welding, masonry and woodworking, and maintenance of textile machinery. Over two years, this programme has produced 242 instructors for industrial training programmes and 347 supervisors for industrial plants.

In Turkey, UNESCO has worked with the Special Fund to establish schools of engineering and architecture at the Middle East Technical University in Ankara. By mid-1962, 65 students had graduated from the engineering school, with bachelor degrees in civil, mechanical, electrical and chemical engineering. Other degrees have been awarded in civil engineering and in mechanical engineering. The school of architecture has conferred over 50 bachelor and master degrees. Among the practical

Metal Trades Training Centre in the United Arab Republic, Egypt, benefits from UNESCO instructors in the gas-welding section.

research activities of the new faculties are studies to improve the water supply and development work to extend communications.

But perhaps the best recent example of how the "multiplier" principle works may be seen in India. The success of India's third Five-Year Plan hinges on the preparation by 1966 of some 750,000 skilled workers for industry. To help meet this critical shortage, the Special Fund and ILO are assisting five Instructor Training Institutes which will be capable of turning out 2,000 graduates a year. These instructors will, in turn, train many more times that number of industrial workers at some 300 industrial training institutes throughout the country. At three of the Instructor Training Institutes—in Calcutta, Madras, and Kanpur—1,500 instructors have already been graduated and 1,000 more are expected to complete their training in 1964. Two other institutes at Hyderabad and Ludhiana are due to open shortly. In courses of nine months duration, instructors are being trained to teach machinists, electricians, mechanics and other factory workers. Several of the international experts are also advising the Government in the planning of its training programmes. In 1963, 15,000 applicants were tested for a variety of trades and a testing programme is in hand for the 1964 intake of apprentices.

RESEARCH AND PLANNING

Apart from the training aspects dealt with above, the Special Fund is equally promoting the establishment of two types of institutes, so necessary in the low-income countries, dealing, respectively, with practical research and with economic planning and development.

Applied research institutes seek for industrial "potentials", as they are called. They help to improve manufacturing techniques, design new equipment and products, and promote better use of local materials, as well as engage in the field work required to raise local productivity.

In Guatemala, for instance, a Central American Research Institute is supported by six governments of the area and supervised by the United Nations. It is promoting industrial growth and economic integration in Central America. New processes have increased the use of local materials, such as in the production of building boards. This Institute has also assisted in as-

94

sessing the financial and technical conditions needed to strengthen business enterprises in Central America.

In Syria, a project is being executed by FAO which has developed better methods of food processing. These techniques have eliminated much waste and have improved market prospects at home and abroad. By similar means, the educational and research stations in Damascus and various demonstration units elsewhere in the country have already doubled profits for figs, apricot pulp, and raisins.

Turning to the other type of institute, which is concerned with planning for development, the Latin American Institute for Economic and Social Planning was opened in Santiago, Chile, in 1962. Seventy-five officials attended the initial training course. Most of them came from government or university service in 19 countries of the region. The Institute gives courses in overall and regional planning for industry, agriculture, transport, and administration, while training courses have so far been conducted in Bolivia, Brazil, Mexico, Paraguay and Uruguay.

A regional planning institute for Asia was approved along the same lines in January 1963. Thus far, twenty-one Asian governments have pledged more than two-thirds of its cash counterpart target of $1.1 million. The United Nations is assisting in preparations for a similar institute in Africa.

IMPACT ON DAILY LIFE

Finally, we can choose from among several such current experiments, a pre-investment project aimed at national development in terms of increased agricultural acreage, to show how the daily lives of millions of ordinary people have been and are being transformed under the Fund's impact.

In the Republic of Korea, some 25 million people are huddled on a narrow coastal strip of arable land. There are only two possibilities for increasing urgently-needed agricultural production: to extend land cultivation of the mountain slopes or to reclaim lands from encroaching seas. Special Fund assistance was sought in carrying out surveys and pilot demonstrations of the agricultural potential in the two areas, both projects being executed by FAO. For a study of the Korean uplands, two watershed drainage basins were selected and land use surveys and groundwater investigations were made.

Two pilot demonstration units of about 4,000 acres were then examined in detail. Extensive experiments were made on the best methods of preventing soil erosion, controlling mountain waters, building small water storage works, and speeding re-forestation. A wide variety of suitable crops and tree species was planted. But perhaps the most important innovation was the introduction of a new form of terracing. This terracing, which slopes into the mountain, has been found effective in preventing soil erosion and storing water. Korean nationals have already been trained in the construction of these terraces, and it is estimated that one million acres of marginal land can be brought under cultivation by this method.

It must be obvious from the foregoing almost random examples of the Fund in action that a new generation of technically equipped and skilled personnel is being brought together in country after country—a trained army of dedicated citizens to fight the *real* war of the Twentieth Century, the war against ignorance and apathy and want.

7

World Trade, The Key

The outstanding accomplishment of the United Nations Development Decade during the year 1964 was undoubtedly the mammoth United Nations Conference on Trade and Development. It was held in Geneva over three months, ending on June 15th.

It had become clear by the beginning of 1964 that the main target laid down for the Development Decade—namely, a minimum growth rate in the developing countries of 5 per cent per annum—would necessitate expansion in the *foreign exchange* earnings of these countries of at least 8 or 9 per cent yearly. This stringent precondition would entail a fundamental break with the experience of the past. What looked like merely a difference of *degree*, on the surface, meant a difference in *kind*, below the surface. If the Development Decade were to succeed, even in its basic aims, the world of the trader and shipper and insurer would never be the same again. That is why the World Trade Conference became so significant an event.

During the past fifteen years or so, the exports of the developing countries (earning their foreign exchange) have increased at the rate of barely 3 per cent each year.* Worse still, the *buying*

---

* The U.N. *Economic Survey* for 1963 pointed to a number of "sources of imbalance" that showed little tendency to lessen. They included up-spiraling living costs in a number of developing countries. Further, despite a "vigorous expansion" in their exports, their rate of growth in 1960-63 continued to lag behind the industrial and centrally-planned economies, and there "has been an even slower growth" in the imports so urgently required for development programmes.

power of their exports over their imports—which they want for their developing programmes—has increased only 2 and a half per cent yearly. No wonder that the growth rate of their economies has been only half that required under the Development Decade!

Shipping, insurance, and freight problems weigh heavily on the developing countries, since they must rely on the services of the traditional seafaring nations, typified by this view of a section of Rotterdam harbour, Netherlands.

Let us look at their problem closer and go back a few years to get our perspective. For exporters of coffee, cocoa, cotton and many other raw materials, the years 1950-62 brought many disappointments. Prices rose and fell, then rose and fell again. Although some advances were made in early 1963, the basic problem remained, namely: *How could world prices be kept on an even keel?*

Most of the world's developing countries depend on foods, fibres, fuels and minerals for their main earnings of foreign exchange. The average value of their exports at the end of the decade of the 1950's was only 1 per cent higher than when the period began. Yet, in the same period, the manufactured goods those same countries *had to buy from abroad* rose in price by an average of 10 per cent. The result has been a "price squeeze" which has sometimes stopped them altogether from importing machinery and other goods so badly needed for their economic and social planning, even before the special drive of the 1960's began. The challenge of this "price squeeze"—i.e. how to close the gap between export earnings and import needs—was one of the leading questions which faced the World Trade Conference.

For three months in the summer of 1964 the European headquarters of the world organization was strained to accommodate the 2,000 delegates and observers who were present from 120 countries. The underlying theme of the long and often heated discussions quickly became apparent: it took charge of the agenda and carried the Conference far beyond what orthodox onlookers expected. It expressed the deeply felt need to adopt a radically new world trade policy, so as to speed the economic development of that two-thirds of the world's population who still live in varying degrees of poverty and want.

The complexity of the problems involved in adapting world trade policies to so many pressing development needs was never underestimated during those twelve weeks of debate. They cannot be adequately dealt with here. It is, nevertheless, the purpose of this chapter to outline as simply as possible some of the general issues with which the Conference grappled, though it is too early yet to assess the impact of the Conference on the Decade as a whole.**

AN ENDURING PARTNERSHIP

Speaker after speaker took the rostrum to recount how the present terms of trade frustrated their economic plans and often completely nullified aid given for this very purpose by the more advanced nations and by the international organizations. Secretary-General U Thant, in opening the Conference, said that this "frustrating phenomenon emphasizes the need to control market forces which have until now been permitted to counter govern-

---

** As this book goes to press before the official reports of the Geneva Trade Conference are available, the "General Principles" recommended by the Conference to govern future trade relations are reproduced in *Appendix 2* to supplement this chapter.

ment policies." Indeed, he added, "the dilemma of our times" was the fundamental need to *reverse* the present trends in trade. It was for this reason that the Conference had been convened.

This was bold language, but the same view was shared by the President of the Conference, Dr. Abdel Moneim El-Kaissouni, Deputy-Prime Minister of the United Arab Republic. "The real need," he declared, "is for a new and vigorous policy of international co-operation, wherein international trade and finance must play a key role in promoting economic development, especially in the less-advanced regions of the world . . . The ultimate aim of the Conference should be to assist in creating an enduring partnership amongst the nations of the world, a partnership through which present inequalities are reduced and mutual assistance is increased."

Dr. Raul Prebisch, of Argentina, the Secretary-General of the Conference, defined the starting point of the Conference as "a clear-cut political concept which has apparently ceased to be a subject of controversy." The prosperous countries of the world cannot neglect the problems of the "economic periphery," where the two-thirds live in very precarious conditions. "Never before" he said, "has there been an opportunity like the present of quickly solving, through contemporary technology, the problem of poverty and its inherent evils in the developing countries. Yet never before have such distressing tensions, as those which beset the developing world, emerged on such a huge scale."

"The developing countries have come to this Conference," the Secretary-General of the Conference pointed out, "with a view to attaining a policy which will enable them to accelerate their rate of economic and social growth and to draw attention to the unavoidable need for a fundamental change in the policy of international co-operation, which must be based on reality."

As the Conference declared in its Final Act, they had assembled "to seek a better and more effective system of international economic co-operation, whereby the division of the world into areas of poverty and plenty may be banished and prosperity achieved by all; and to find ways by which the human and material resources of the world may be harnessed for the abolition of poverty everywhere. In an age when scientific progress has put unprecedented abundance within man's reach, it is essential that

100

the flows of world trade should help to eliminate the wide economic disparities among nations. The international community must combine its efforts to ensure that all countries—regardless of size, of wealth, of economic and social system—enjoy the benefits of international trade for their economic development and social progress."

MAIN LINES OF ACTION

To meet the problem of the perpetual trade imbalance, the main lines of action could be summed up under six points; and these topics came up again and again in the weeks which followed:

(1) *Primary commodities* should be given easier access in the markets of the industrial countries;

(2) *Export earnings* of developing countries should be increased and stabilized;

(3) *Restrictions* hampering the entry of manufactures and semi-manufactures of developing countries should give way to a preferential policy;

(4) *Formation of groups* of developing countries should help each other to share imports between them;

(5) *Socialist countries* should encourage trade on a long-term basis;

(6) *External debts* should be "serviced" at lower rates and the cost of freight and insurance should be lowered.

It is true that, in working out the details of these and related principles of trade, the discussions were often technical, but some of the chief arguments and conclusions can be summarized below, although it will not be necessary in this brief review to classify them under the formal divisions of the Conference agenda.***

There was, for instance, almost universal recognition of the necessity, stated above, to ensure a more stable market at a fair price level for basic commodities on which so many of the developing countries depended for their foreign exchange and for the import of manufactures. At the same time, as these countries move forward industrially, another need arises for the opening up of new markets for their infant industries. It is against the

***A condensed version of the subject matter and action taken by the Conference was issued by the UN Office of Public Information in July 1964.

101

background of these two considerations that methods and machinery to help finance an expansion of international trade were debated.

There was a large measure of agreement that ways and means must be devised to secure fair prices for primary commodities originating in the developing countries. The primary commodity market must be organized in such a way as to ensure a price level high enough to be comparable to the prices of manufactured goods which that country had to buy. How else could a country balance its terms of trade? This was especially true of countries dependent on one or only a few basic products for their foreign exchange. It was pointed out that the most important single factor which could help them to keep straight their payments position would be to increase their export earnings through better prices.

One African speaker explained that if the price of a basic food commodity, produced within his country, could be pegged at $250 per ton—which would be only half the 1954 price of $500 per ton—its *income* from this product would nevertheless be increased by at least $20 million a year—over a seven year period by more than $140 million—thus enabling the country to finance a sizeable portion of its seven-year Development Plan. This would also have the effect of reducing the country's reliance on foreign aid. But could an exporting country induce its wealthy customers to stick to an agreed price over a reasonable period of time?

STANDSTILL ON BARRIERS

The Latin-American countries suffered particularly as a result of the "gap" between prices for their primary commodities and the manufactured goods they had to buy. Agricultural products, from both tropical and temperate zones, together with their minerals and fuels, were experiencing downward price fluctuations in the world markets. Moreover, tariff restrictions were preventing Latin-American products from competing in international trade. So what was the use of offering them "aid" with one hand, and taking away their livelihood with the other?

What was the response of the industrialized countries to all this? On the subject of primary commodities, France favoured

102

freedom of trade with a better organization of markets. New commodity agreements should be negotiated, the French delegate agreed, particularly for primary commodities, and higher prices should be paid for tropical products, thus raising the export earnings of the producer countries. Another leading industrial power, the United Kingdom, proposed a "standstill on new barriers" to the trade of the less-developed countries. The proposal urged the removal of duties on tropical and primary products imported from developing countries. New international agreements should cover access to markets, as well as the level of prices, and prices should be stabilized at remunerative levels so as to encourage development of new markets. The United States representative held that the industrial countries must be prepared to reduce tariffs and other barriers and to import primary products. Advanced trading countries should co-operate "whenever feasible" in perfecting arrangements to reduce instabilities. But these problems could be usefully approached only on a commodity-by-commodity basis. There could be no blanket concessions.

The countries of Eastern Europe were in general agreement with the need for the stabilization of commodity prices. They declared their sympathy with the desire of the developing countries to find ways for the elimination or reduction of the damage caused to their economies by fluctuations in both demand and prices. These factors, they asserted, characterized present world capitalist markets. The Communist countries specifically mentioned the likelihood of their increased requirements for such products as cocoa, tea, tropical agricultural products, vegetable oils, cotton, jute, and certain mineral ores. This expansion would be presumably accompanied by corresponding increases in purchases by the developing countries of goods from Eastern Europe. Such policies could best be carried out under the terms of bilateral, long-term trade agreements that would ensure permanent markets and so contribute to the steady growth in the exchange of goods.

At the end of the debate on the problems facing the commodity trade of developing countries, the Conference recommended a number of provisions aimed at increasing the export earnings of these countries. They included measures for stimulating "a

103

dynamic and steady growth and ensuring reasonable predictability in the real export earnings of the developing countries so as to provide them with expanding resources for their economic and social development, while taking into account the interests of consumers in importing countries, through remunerative, equitable and stable prices for primary commodities." Other provisions would cover "measures and actions for the removal of obstacles (tariff, non-tariff and other) and discriminatory practices."

Argentina's new National Steel Works is rising from the pampas on the Parana River. UN technical assistance behind the steel programme has been concerned with the study of Argentine raw materials—iron ore, coal, and manganese. As UN assistance proceeds, it will become possible to use larger and larger proportions of local materials.

The Conference also wanted to see a commission on commodity arrangements and policies within the framework of the continuing machinery (referred to below) to be established as a result of the Conference. Interestingly enough, too, the Conference expressed the belief that "food aid" should become an integral part of international aid under the United Nations and FAO. Furthermore, it recommended special action, both national and international, to deal with cases where natural products exported by developing countries were facing competition from synthetics and other substitutes.

ENCOURAGING INFANT MANUFACTURES

It was recognized that, in the long run, the development of manufactured goods of their own provided the best means for strengthening the economies of "new" countries and for adding to their earnings of foreign exchange. To accomplish this, the infant industries of the developing countries required assistance of different kinds. Moreover, outlets for their products had to be sought in the markets of the industrialized countries. This, of course, raised big difficulties. It was emphasized that the industrialized countries should grant trade preferences—that is, concessions in relation to the goods of advanced countries—to the developing countries, at least for an agreed list of manufactures.

All developed countries were accordingly urged to reduce or eliminate duties on manufactured and semi-manufactured products of developing countries. "Market economy" countries were asked to encourage their industrialists to seek investment opportunities in the developing countries, and to promote integrated manufacturing between developing and developed countries. Countries with centrally-planned economies told the Conference that they were willing to increase the import of manufactures from the developing countries and also to use the funds they thus received in repayment of credits given to the developing countries.

Latin-American countries, in particular, called for a clear pronouncement of general principles for a *new structure of international trade*. (See Appendix 2.) This should be founded upon a non-discriminatory treatment in favour of all developing countries, with a list of the concessions that they hoped to obtain from the industrialized countries. They asked for guarantees from the industrial countries concerning access for Latin-American products to the latter's markets on a non-discriminatory basis. They believed that the time had come when the industries in Latin America should become part and parcel of the dynamic industrial processes of modern nations, instead of being left outside like pariahs.

But more positive action was needed to promote industrial dynamism. Hence, the Conference called on the United Nations General Assembly to "take suitable action with a view to the establishment of a specialized agency for industrial development". Among the functions of the proposed agency would be to publish information concerning industrial technology, to assist the regional planning of industrial development in developing countries, to offer advice and to cooperate in the training of the staff needed for such industrial development.

A NEW ORGANIZATION?

The question of preferences brought up the position of GATT. But what is GATT?

To go back to the beginning, the Bretton Woods Conference in 1944 had proposed an International Trade Organization (ITO) which would draw up rules of fair trade and help to reduce barriers that hinder the flow of goods and services around the world. The proposed agency never came into being, but some of its objectives have since been included in an international commercial treaty, known as the General Agreement on Trade and Tariffs (GATT). Thirty-seven Governments, accounting for some eighty per cent of world trade, have signed this Treaty. The staff appointed to an Interim Commission of ITO became the secretariat of GATT. The United Nations co-operates with the member nations through this secretariat, and the International Monetary Fund also works closely with it. Although much more has yet to be done, some advance has been made through GATT from time to time in reducing or eliminating foreign exchange restrictions which hamper world trade.

Among the Asian and African countries there was broad agreement that the present machinery under GATT had failed to respond to the vital needs of the developing countries or to provide a satisfactory instrument to promote their trade in the desired directions. While many speakers favoured the establishment of a new trade organization under the aegis of the United Nations and with universal membership—which was what ITO was *intended* to be twenty years ago—there was a general recognition that such machinery might prove too ambitious at the present time.

Support for a remodelled GATT, that would function as a more effective instrument of international trade for the benefit of all the countries of the world, was likewise forthcoming. But if GATT could not be suitably expanded and altered, many countries indicated that they would then favour the creation of a new agency better suited to changing world conditions and to the pressing needs of developed and developing countries alike.

There was wide agreement between the Latin-American countries, for instance, for the establishment of adequate machinery to ensure compliance with the Conference's decisions. One way to do this would be to keep in existence the present Conference on Trade and Development as a regular and permanent feature of the United Nations, with its own Secretariat and Standing Committee. As a group, the countries of this region did not favour the establishment of any new international trade organization at the present time. Rather, they were in support of adapting existing machinery to make it more responsive to the problems of developing countries.

The countries of Eastern Europe, on the other hand, maintained that it was necessary to establish a universal trade organization under the auspices of the United Nations to deal with the whole complex of world trade, in which all countries concerned would participate. The new organization would have as its principal task the promotion of international trade as an instrument of economic progress. It should also become a centre for co-ordinating the activities of other United Nations bodies in the field of trade, and might also be responsible for ensuring the implementation of the Conference decisions.

The final recommendations of the Conference on this important question of future organisation are summarized at the end of this chapter.

WHAT IS "INVISIBLE" TRADE?

On the difficult subject of financing economic development, emphasis was again and again placed on the need of the developing countries for a greater flow of capital on longer terms and at lower interest rates, if industrialization were to move forward. Economic assistance should *not* be tied to individual projects in the recipient country or to the purchases of required equipment abroad, as is generally the case at present (see Chapter 6). The possibilities of greater financial aid resulting from all-round disarmament was never absent from the minds of the impoverished countries. The diversion for the purpose of development of at least a percentage of funds now being devoted to the arms race made economic as well as moral sense.

Afro-Asian representatives also looked to the Conference to take action in the field of "invisible trade"—meaning the heavy shipping rates, insurance costs, freight and other charges which contribute to the growing balance-of-payments difficulties of the developing countries. Obviously, the advanced trading nations have a monopoly of these essential services; in fact, they have had several centuries start! Shipping goods to developing countries at high freight rates is bad enough; but exports from these countries suffer an even greater burden. Hence, the "invisible" earnings of most of them are very small, while the drain of foreign exchange to meet payments on the shipping and insurance charges imposed by the wealthier countries is excessively high.

This dilemma might eventually be met by the developing countries establishing their own shipping services. Meantime, the lowering of freight charges by the major commercial powers and the expansion of insurance services in the developing countries on a national or regional basis—as well as the encouragement of tourism—would give them needed foreign exchange. The developing countries should also take from now on a more effective part in decisions relating to the terms and charges for sea and air transport in an effort to bring freight-rate charges under a more equitable control and thus halt practices which are impeding the development of merchant fleets in the less-developed regions.

Such problems need only be stated in this bald and summary fashion for it to be apparent that the 1964 Conference scratched the surface of a massive amalgam of national and commercial interests which would not yield to easy or early solutions.

The topic of tourism, however, seemed to inspire both present confidence and optimism in the near future. Developed countries were urged to grant financial and technical assistance in this field and to facilitate both public and private investment for that purpose, as well as to remove obstacles to tourism, such as currency restrictions, customs regulations, and taxes. They should also promote group travel to the developing countries. For their part, developing countries were advised to integrate tourism into their development plans, and to create favourable conditions for

108

foreign investments in tourism. The Conference urged that organizations assisting the developing countries should consider grants or long-term loans to tourist industries, hotels, and similar ventures and especially to assist the conservation and utilization of archeological, historical, and natural sites in the developing countries.

REGIONAL GROUPINGS ARE FAVOURED

Regional economic groupings were seen to offer many opportunities for strengthening commercial relations and to enlarge markets for the products of most developing countries. For example, present barriers to trade among developing countries, such as the diversity of systems of payment and customs practices, could be broken down by this means, and there could be a considerable increase in trade between neighbouring countries.

Special privileges granted within a given economic group, however, should not adversely affect the position of third parties. This the Conference wanted to make clear. In fact, there was specific opposition to what was called inward-looking groupings, which adopted policies detrimental to the interests of third parties, thus disrupting the traditional patterns of trade, and creating obstacles for traditional exporters in the markets of the member countries.

The countries of Western Europe, and particularly members of the European Economic Community—the Common Market—were convinced that regional cooperation would be likely to have the most beneficial effects for developing countries. It was pointed out, however, that such groupings of developing countries could not be formed without the consent and support of the industrialized countries, which ought in return to agree to discrimination against their own exports for the benefit of the new areas.

The desirability of expanding markets through increased trade with the centrally-planned economies as also discussed, at the same time developing closer relations with countries at different stages of development and with other regional groupings. This concept of stimulating trade among countries at different levels of development and with different political systems, was widely endorsed. Valuable contributions to the implementation of this idea could be seen in such projects as a regional highway programme, a telecommunications network, and schemes for electrical interconnections.

Significant for the development of international economic relations, according to a number of Eastern European representatives, was the early attainment of general and complete disarmament. This would allow the freeing of huge material resources, now wasted in the form of military expenditure, for the benefit of mankind as a whole and particularly for those living in the developing countries of Asia, Africa and Latin America.

Under this head, passing reference can be made to the special difficulties of the 23 participants in the Conference that qualified as "land-locked" countries, and who wished to enjoy free and unrestricted transit rights over their neighbours' territories to the sea. It was generally agreed that this was a right which should be recognized by law and be embodied in a new international convention—a duty falling on the follow-up organ of the Conference.

WHAT OF THE FUTURE?

As stated earlier, many delegations wanted a United Nations Trade organisation to be set up which would do for them all what GATT had had apparently failed to do for any nation. The Conference therefore recommended that the UN General Assembly should do three things:

(a) establish the Conference on Trade and Development as an organ of the General Assembly,

(b) establish a Trade and Development Board as the permanent organ of the Conference itself, and

(c) provide a permanent full-time secretariat for servicing the Conference and its subsidiary bodies.

It was not thought, however, that these plans should prevent participating governments from making the most effective use of existing institutions; but, at the same time, there should be a further review of present and proposed arrangements in the light of experience.

The Conference, further, took note of "the widespread desire among developing countries for a comprehensive trade organization," and recognized that permanent institutional arrangements were necessary to continue the work initiated by the Conference and to implement its recommendations. The Conference would be convened at intervals of not more than three years, and its next session will be held in early 1966. Its membership would comprise all states which are members of the United Nations, the specialized agencies, or the International Atomic Energy Agency. In following up the work of the 1964 gathering, the Conference would also help to coordinate United Nations activities in the field of trade, and initiate action to further new trade conventions.

AN APPEAL BY 77 DEVELOPING COUNTRIES

At the conclusion of the Conference, 77 developing nations issued a joint declaration in which they declared that the 1964 event marked "the beginning of a new era in the evolution of international cooperation for trade and development." The declaration added:

> "Such cooperation must serve as a decisive instrument for ending the division of the world into areas of affluence and intolerable poverty. This task is the outstanding challenge of our times. The injustice and neglect of centuries needs to be redressed. The developing countries are united in their resolve to continue the quest for such redress and look to the entire international community for understanding and support in this endeavour."

The developing countries made it clear that they considered the final recommendations of the Conference as only an initial step towards the endorsement of *a new trade policy for development*. Progress so far made in economic development was not at all adequate. For example, they believed that there was not sufficient appreciation of the problem of the "trade gap," and that only the "most limited approaches" had so far been made to improve trade in primary commodities or give preferences for exports of manufactures. Nevertheless, the concluding declaration stated that the developing countries "accepted the results of this Conference in the hope that these results would lay the foundation for more substantial progress in the period ahead . . . in recognition of the need for a cooperative effort in the international field."

111

8

Work In Progress

The citizens of Chryssoupolis in Eastern Greece were not rich, though the name of their town means "Gold Town." In 1955, the Greek Government decided to make Chryssoupolis the site of an experiment in village development and asked the United Nations to help them. Chryssoupolis is a market town and every Wednesday the people from the surrounding countryside come to buy and sell and to exchange the latest gossip with their friends. The large square near the church is packed with carts carrying fodder, particularly alfalfa, hay and grain from the plains.

When the townsfolk heard of the new project there was great excitement. A United Nations expert arrived, and a meeting of the Town Council was called. He explained that what the Government wanted was to make Chryssoupolis a model of what a modern community should be like and what it could do for its inhabitants if properly organized. The transformation was to be planned by the people themselves, but carried out under the guidance of the United Nations expert.

The inhabitants talked about the ways to cooperate with the Government services and how to contribute their labour and some of their own money. They were asked to suggest the most important pieces of development they thought they should start off with. This meant, among other things, finding the best means to increase production. It involved spending time and money on irrigation, improved animal stock and machines for agriculture. After these objectives were examined, came a discussion on technical training, which many people in the village considered most important of all, for improving work-skills was basic to everything else.

The first task was to make a short-term plan, while long-term plans were being evolved. As a matter of fact, before the mission arrived, some irrigation work had been commenced; but it had not got very far, as the villagers were unwilling to use their own money for something which seemed beyond their capacity to complete. The Government now decided to make some money available for this work, and the United Nations provided a tractor and a land-rover. So work on the irrigation project started again and a development plan was got under way. It was really based on the ideas put up by the people themselves. It became clear that it was in their own interests that it was being devised; they realized that they would be the beneficiaries, so they put their hearts into it.

Since those early days, roads have been made, the irrigation scheme extended, more houses built, and electricity supplied to the township. Future plans include the formation of co-operative marketing societies, the building of an animal clinic, a crafts centre and a health centre, and better educational facilities.

All this goes to show what just *one man can do*, when he is welcomed and is able to bring to a village—or to a town or a country—what the people themselves *want*, if only they are shown how to get it.

We have seen this principle at work again and again in the foregoing pages. In this chapter, starting with Europe, we can make a round-the-world selection from the crowded work-in-progress sheet of the UN and its agencies, especially in so far as the separate functions enumerated in earlier chapters can be seen to interlock in this constantly-expanding programme of UN assistance.

AFRICA RESURGENT

From this one-man initiative in Europe, we now turn to examine, by way of contrast, the activities of the Civilian Operations in the Congo, where the United Nations has provided the largest programme of technical assistance for any one country in the history of the world Organization. The Congo conflict has been

113

told[1] in various ways, but chiefly in terms of the violent struggle to maintain the political integrity of that vast territory; so much so that the astonishing miracle of economic and social transformation that the whole UN family, working together, has brought about in the course of barely three years, has been largely overlooked.

The last annual report of the Civilian Operations Office in Leopoldville (issued in May 1964) shows that 631 experts and technicians of 48 nationalities were provided by the United Nations and its agencies in a score of fields, covering education, health, agriculture, communications, mining and other resources, basic economic and social development, and the judiciary. In addition, UNESCO helped recruit over 800 secondary school teachers. The first 55 Congolese doctors trained abroad under WHO have returned home and their presence will soon allow a reduction in the number of foreign doctors provided by WHO. This process of replacing international by Congolese personnel will, however, take some years to complete. In the meantime, there will be a continuing need for large numbers of experts and technicians, both executive and advisory; but it is hoped that the cost of such personnel can increasingly be charged to the Congo's national budget, so that international aid can be concentrated in its traditional areas of advisory services and training.

The results of these UN activities have been indeed striking. Secondary school enrolment in the Congo rose to 85,000 students in 1963 (compared with 28,900 in 1959). To make this increase possible, further teachers were recruited from 29 countries with UNESCO's aid. Others have been provided through bilateral aid and by religious organizations and, in all, some 3,300 internationally recruited teachers are working in the Congo in the current school year. A comparable annual increase is expected to go on until 1967. UNESCO also sent mobile teams into 14 areas to offer advance training to some 1,600 primary school teachers in their own localities. Vehicles, audio-visual aids and other supplies were provided by UNICEF. Other UNESCO experts have worked with the Congolese Government in staffing teacher-training institutions,

[1] See panphlet: *The United Nations and the Congo*, United Nations, New York, 1963.

114

obtaining imported textbooks, and organizing courses for Ministry of Education personnel.

In the health field, WHO provided 174 doctors and technicians for work in 74 hospitals and nine other institutions. Yet the need is still such that more than 40 hospitals of at least 100 beds each were functioning without a single doctor at the end of 1963. In addition, WHO personnel have worked to prevent the spread of outbreaks of smallpox and other diseases and to improve community hygiene. They have waged anti-mosquito campaigns to combat malaria, which is described as the most prevalent of diseases in the Congo. Health centres have been opened in major cities and the Ministry of Health is planning long-range development of health services under WHO guidance.

In the agricultural field, twenty-six experts from FAO, for example, have worked to expand tea and coffee cultivation, protect livestock from diseases, control exploitation of forests, and improve fishing. An FAO poultry centre was set up for training,

UNESCO operated in the Congo from the earliest days of the crisis and provided teachers and educational administrators to shore up the country's educational structure.

and other training provided for personnel, ranging from farm mechanics to agronomists.

In the courts of the chief cities, nearly 50 international jurists and magistrates have been recruited by the United Nations to serve as judges and attorneys. Again, this number is far from sufficient, for, of the 31 district courts, 15 are still without magistrates. Training in law is being provided at a number of institutions, with United Nations aid; and it is anticipated that graduates will be available by 1966 to fill positions of the magistracy. Other UN experts, attached to the Ministry of Justice, have advised on police and prison reforms and drawn up a revision of the legal code.

Civil aviation, meteorology, telecommunications, postal services, and surface transportation have been handled by the appropriate UN agencies. Air transport plays a very important part in the Congo's economic life. In 1963, the International Civil Aviation Organization (ICAO) provided essential ground services at eight major airports, including technical work by international radio-operators and mechanics.

The World Meteorological Organization, another United Nations agency, has provided international personnel for weather services, so essential to civil aviation, training Congolese forecasters and observers; and other services are being expanded with the aid of experts from the International Telecommunication Union (ITU); and ITU experts are helping as well in training Congolese operating and maintenance personnel.

A big step forward in the social welfare field was the establishment of a Community Development Fund to help local groups raise living standards. Through this difficult period of conflict and reconstruction (1960-64), UN personnel have been present in all the major centres helping with basic economic planning, labour legislation, developing natural resources, and, above all, training Congolese nationals to serve their "new" country in the customs, taxation, and other administrative fields.

In fact, training has formed a major element of the United Nations Civilian Operations. UN fellowships enabled 1,300 Congolese to study in 1963 in their own country at national institutes in such fields as law, education, mining, civil aviation, meteorology, public works, agriculture, social work, and health. For specialized training not available in the Congo, 47 overseas fellowships were also provided.

It should be noted finally that the greater part of these "civilian operations" were financed by the UN Congo Fund, and that contributions to it from 16 Governments have totalled about $44 million; but the Congolese Government itself has made an additional contribution of $11 million to cover local costs. During 1963, the UN technical assistance took over the financing of part of the work described above. In addition, the Special Fund has financed one of the training institutes and planned to finance two more.

The above account of what is being achieved in a single African nation has been given in some detail, not solely because it represents the biggest technical assistance programme yet attempted by the UN for any one country, but also because it presents to the world—if the workaday world has eyes to see it—a shining example of supranational co-operation at its best.

A WORLD NETWORK

Although the purpose of this chapter is primarily to supplement by a few practical examples, such as the above, the basic principles underlying the economic and technical aid described in earlier chapters, our story would be by no means complete if the growing value to all developing countries of the *Regional* Economic Commissions were to be ignored. There exist four of these and a few paragraphs devoted to the work of at least three of them—in Africa, Asia, and Latin America—would serve to emphasize the fact that no developing country today is acting in isolation from its neighbours.

The UN's system of Regional Economic Commissions will play an increasing role during the next phase of the Development Decade. In fact, the formation of a regional Commission for Africa in April, 1958, was acclaimed in the Secretary-General's annual report as "an important step forward and a recognition of the growing importance of regional co-operation in economic and social development programs for the peoples of Africa." And the Secretary-General continued:

"Almost from the very outset of the life of the United Nations, the Economic and Social Council had begun the

117

creation of regional commissions, starting with Europe and Asia and the Far East and later adding Latin America. The expansion of the regional commissions system is clearly related to a trend that has made itself felt in our work. . . . By promoting concerned inter-governmental action and a continuous exchange have rendered services that have become increasingly appreciated by the participating governments and have reinforced the technical assistance that the Organization has been able to lend to underdeveloped countries."[2]

This network of regional economic commissions now comprises the Economic Commission for Europe (ECE), the Economic Commission for Asia and the Far East (ECAFE), the Economic Commission for Latin America (ECLA), and the Economic Commission for Africa (ECA). The basic functions of all the regional economic commissions are identical, in that their aim is to assist in raising the level of economic activity in their respective regions, and to strengthen the economic relations of the countries in each region both among themselves and with other countries of the world. To achieve this underlying aim the commissions undertake investigations and studies of economic and technological problems, and the collection and dissemination of economic and statistical information. Provision is also made for the participation in the work of each commission of members of the United Nations that are not members of the commission concerned.

Naturally, the commissions ensure that their work is co-ordinated with that of other organs of the United Nations and with the Specialized Agencies. The secretaries of these commissions are, in fact, integral parts of the Secretariat as a whole. The staff of each commission is composed of personnel from the countries in its respective region, as well as from other member states.

The Economic Commission for Africa, which we shall notice first, has 35 members and eleven associate members, and among the latter are four European states that have responsibilities in Africa. The Commission has its headquarters in Addis Ababa and its sessions are representative gatherings of high-ranking government officials and experts. The training in particular of economists, statisticians and administrators, occupies an important place in their work program. A good deal of the Commission's

2 See pamphet: *Co-operation for Economic Progress,* United Nations, New York, 1960.

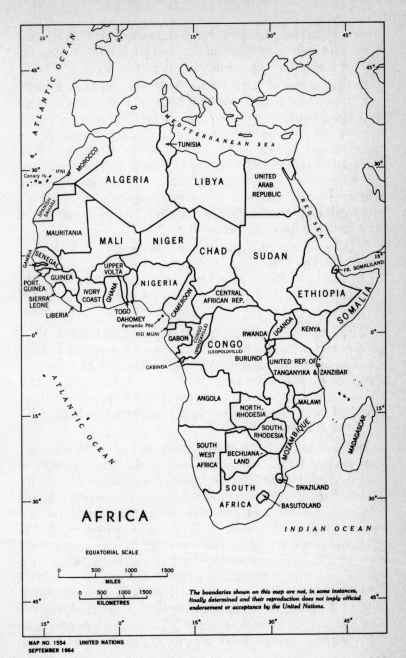

AFRICA

EQUATORIAL SCALE

MILES
0   500   1000   1500

KILOMETRES
0   500   1000   1500

The boundaries shown on this map are not, in some instances,
finally determined and their reproduction does not imply official
endorsement or acceptance by the United Nations.

MAP NO. 1554   UNITED NATIONS
SEPTEMBER 1964

119

other work has been concerned with studies and advisory services in the field of development planning and project formulation, the need of which has been particularly urgent in Africa.

The promotion of intra-African trade has also been a major task of the Commission. The dependence of African countries for their foreign exchange on their primary products is intensified by the fact that individual African countries usually depend on the export of one or two products (for instance, Ghana on cocoa, Ethiopia on coffee, Sudan on cotton). And, since agriculture is the mainstay of African economic life, one of the other main concerns of the Commission is to improve agricultural production and marketing. Hence, close co-operation has been established with FAO and the other UN agencies.

But the considerable distance yet to be travelled between promise and performance is evident from two recent assessments by U Thant and Mr. Eugene Black, respectively. Addressing the African "Summit" Conference in Cairo on 17 July 1964, the UN Secretary-General said:

"Africa has always had a special position in relation to those programmes of the United Nations, which are designed to assist the developing countries in their stupendous task of promoting the economic and social progress of their peoples. I believe that the vast riches of the continent, some of which have already been exploited, are sufficient to provide in time rising standards of living for all Africans."

The need to develop the natural resources of Africa was similarly stressed by the former President of the World Bank, who described the contrast between Africa's resource potential and the present state of development as staggering. He pointed out that, while a series of dams over the Congo River could produce electric power capital equal to all the electric power installed in Western Europe, the only economic activity of the inhabitants of that almost deserted area appeared to be the collection of a species of edible caterpillar. In one of the poorest corners of Africa he saw one of the richest iron deposits in the world. Referring to the place of entrepreneurship and management in this vast undertaking, he confessed that "the continent's major economic enterprises remain today completely dominated by foreign-

ers—by Europeans, Lebanese, Syrians, Indians, practically any-
body except Africans."[3]

HIGHWAY TO THE FUTURE

Similarly, the main task of the Economic Commission for Asia
and the Far East (ECAFE) is to further the overall economic
development of that variegated region. Through its subsidiary
bodies ECAFE deals with practically all important branches of
Asian economic life: development and planning, economic research, finance, transport and communications, flood control and
waters resources, industries and mineral resources, trade, housing,
and social aspects of economic development. Work in these fields
is carried out through meetings and seminars and research. The
Commission has twenty-six members and two associate members.

During the 1950's, Asian countries began strenuous efforts to
break through the economic stagnation that had long held their
vast populations in poverty. This marked a significant change
from passive acceptance of low standards of living to a determi-
nation to raise them by creating the conditions for economic
growth. Much was achieved during that decade. But these
achievements were not enough to effect any substantial improvement in the average real incomes of most Asian countries, as we
have seen. The decision of the United Nations, therefore, to make
the 1960's a Development Decade has had a special appeal to the
ECAFE region.

Although many of the countries in the region achieved their
political independence only after the Second World War, and
are sometimes referred to as "young" countries, these newly
independent countries are now passing through an important
phase in their history. On the one hand, they have to retrace their
bearings to their old national traditions and culture, and on the
other hand they have to take their rightful places as members of
an international community and participate fully in the dynamic
progress of the modern world. "Entrusted with the great task of
assisting the countries of the region in their efforts to reconstruct
and develop their economies, ECAFE has set its work in the his-

3 Quoted from statement by Robert K. A. Gardiner, Executive-Secretary of
ECA, 20 February, 1964.

toric and human context of the region it serves. A determined beginning has been made to expedite the development of Asian economies and to proceed in a systematic may with furthering industry and trade and making long-overdue improvements in agriculture, transport and communications and social services."[4]

Partly as a result of the work of ECAFE and other international organizations, there is now in the region a general recognition of the value of sharing experiences on a regional, as well as an international basis. There is a growing trend in the region for economic development to proceed through co-operative effort, not only by countries of the region, but also in concert with the industrially-advanced nations of the West. The Executive-Secretary of ECAFE makes the further interesting observation that: "ECAFE regards the many regional projects which it undertakes or assists not merely as measures for providing technical aid to member countries, but also as means of promoting regional consciousness and stepping up regional co-operation."

Examples of this are the preparation of the first regional oil and natural gas maps of Asia and the Far East yet to be made; the setting up of Regional Housing Centres at Bandung and New Delhi, the Petroleum Training Institute in Iran, and the Asian Institute for Economic Development and Planning at Bangkok; the comprehensive programme for developing the Lower Mekong Basin (referred to below); and the project for developing the Asian Highway. This great highway will one day make it possible for people to travel by road from Saigon and Singapore to Teheran and onward to Europe.

ECAFE is by no means just a forum and a clearing-house for information, nor is it merely a fact-finding body and a centre for economic analysis. One of its essential functions is to make recommendations for governmental and inter-governmental *action*. It also provides, on request, expert advice and assistance to governments who wish to make economic changes. Here are a few examples of such action:—

---

[4] Quoted from statement by V. Nyun, Executive-Secretary of ECAFE, *Helping Economic Development in Asia and the Far East*, United Nations, New York, 1964

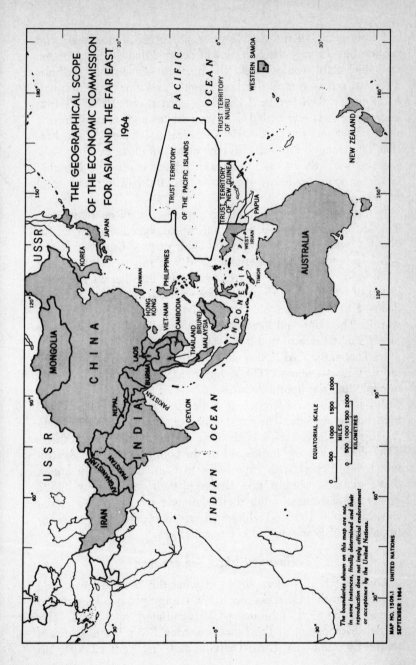

THE GEOGRAPHICAL SCOPE
OF THE ECONOMIC COMMISSION
FOR ASIA AND THE FAR EAST
1964

PACIFIC

OCEAN

WESTERN SAMOA

TRUST TERRITORY
OF THE PACIFIC ISLANDS

TRUST TERRITORY
OF NAURU

TRUST TERRITORY
OF NEW GUINEA

WEST
IRIAN   PAPUA

NEW ZEALAND

USSR

USSR

MONGOLIA

CHINA

KOREA

JAPAN

TAIWAN

HONG KONG

PHILIPPINES

VIET-NAM

CAMBODIA

LAOS

BURMA

THAILAND

BRUNEI
MALAYSIA

NEPAL

INDIA

PAKISTAN

AFGHANISTAN

PAKISTAN

IRAN

CEYLON

INDONESIA

TIMOR

AUSTRALIA

INDIAN   OCEAN

EQUATORIAL SCALE

0   500   1000   1500   2000
MILES

0   500 1000 1500 2000
KILOMETRES

*The boundaries shown on this map are not,
in some instances, finally determined and their
reproduction does not imply official endorsement
or acceptance by the United Nations.*

MAP NO. 1509.1   UNITED NATIONS
SEPTEMBER 1964

123

Burma is one of the world's main producers of rice, teak, and rubber; but recently the government decided that the construction of a steel plant would benefit the Burmese economy as a whole. This was a new venture for that country and much research had to be undertaken before it could be carried out. ECAFE's iron and steel expert was called in to give advice and, in co-operation with (what was then) the UN Technical Assistance Administration, he arranged for Burmese technicians to make first-hand observations in iron and steel plants in Japan. As a result, valuable changes were made in the plans for Burma's nascent steel industry.

In the Philippines weaving is an important small-scale industry. The old handlooms used in the farmsteads had not changed for about a hundred years, producing cloth varying from two to ten yards in length. But modern demand was for a cloth-length of forty yards or more, so ECAFE gathered together in Manila a group of expert loom designers from various countries and they decided to widen the old loom and to introduce an automatic shuttle. The improved looms proved so successful that they have now found their way to other Asian countries.

In Thailand ECAFE was able to assist lignite production for industrial development. The government was naturally interested in exploiting the lignite deposits and when ECAFE organized in Tokyo a regional conference on mineral resources, lignite ranked high on the agenda. The Conference organized a study tour to Australia, to investigate operations in the lignite mines there. Thai officials were so impressed by the competence of an Australian lignite expert with experience in Germany's lignite mines, that they invited him to take charge of their newly set-up lignite power organization. A big thermal power station is now under construction in Thailand which will furnish economically a plentiful supply of power to the needy provinces.

INTERNATIONAL RIVER PROJECT

To conclude this short survey of what the Decade means and *can* mean to the Asian people, a few paragraphs can be devoted to one of the most ambitious projects initiated by ECAFE. This is the development of the Lower Mekong River Basin, which is shared by Cambodia, Laos, Thailand and Viet-Nam. ECAFE has

124

been instrumental in bringing the four riparian countries together, in securing enthusiastic backing from other countries to assist in the development of this international river basin, supported by the international organizations within the United Nations family. Indeed, the Mekong Project (about which some details were given in Chapter 6) is a unique effort in the history of international co-operation.

The technical possibilities for the large-scale multi-purpose development of the river's lower basin, led to the organization in 1956 of a team of high-ranking international experts to conduct a comprehensive field survey of the main river. Their report outlined the possibilities for developing hydro-electric power, irrigation, navigation, and flood control at six sites on the main river. Realizing the importance of the Mekong's development to the improvement of their economy, the four riparian countries established, under the aegis of the United Nations, a Committee for Co-ordination of Investigations of the Lower Mekong Basin, composed of representatives of the four countries, serviced by a United Nations secretariat. The Committee's first action was to request the United Nations to send a second group of international experts to review the studies and to make specific recommendations on the next steps to be taken. This mission laid down a five-year multi-purpose programme of studies essential for the sound planning of the project, at a total cost of about $9 million.

As the four riparian countries tackled the task of taming the river, financial and technical assistance flowed to them from many quarters. France announced in 1957 that it was placing the equivalent of $100,000 at the disposal of the Committee. Within a year, the Committee's resources exceeded $4 million; and by mid-1963 they had grown to over $37 million. Since 1959, when engineers and equipment first began to move on to key sites in the Mekong basin, field operations have proceeded with growing momentum. Hydrologic stations have been established; aerial mapping of the main stream and tributaries areas has been carried out, and the work of levelling the main river has already been completed. The first five-year programme of investigations has been virtually completed, after only four years; and a second five-year investigation programme, expected to cost about $21 million, has been drawn up.

An extensive survey of the lower Mekong River basin, for the benefit of the four riprarian countries—Laos, Thailand, Cambodia and Viet-Nam—has been conducted under the auspices of the United Nations Economic Commission for Asia and the Far East (ECAFE), with the active backing of Australia, Canada, France, India, Iran, Japan, New Zealand, the United Kingdom and the United States, as well as the UN and several of its agencies.

At the same time, "investigation" has become "investment." With the help of loans of $11 million from the Federal Republic of Germany (as mentioned earlier) and $6 million from the Thai Government, funds have been secured for the first construction work. This will be a dam and power station with transmission lines on one of the Mekong tributaries in northeastern Thailand. Finance is also available for construction to begin on a second tributary project in Thailand. To date, sixteen countries, eleven United Nations agencies, three foundations, and three private companies, as well as the four riparian states, are participating in this complex international venture. Resources of manpower, equipment, training facilities or materials, and investment capital have been made available or pledged by Australia, Canada, China, the Federal Republic of Germany, France, India, Iran, Israel, Italy, Japan, the Netherlands, New Zeland, Pakistan, the Philippines, the United Kingdom, and the United States. Is not this becoming a normal pattern of the One World of the future?

A NOTION WHICH DIES HARD

Since the economic development of Latin-America and the raising of the standard of living of its population are basic aims of the Economic Commission for Latin America, most of its effort has been concentrated in these fields. ECLA has 27 members, and two associate members, and its headquarters are in Santiago, Chile. According to Raúl Prebisch, ECLA's Executive-Secretary for many years: "The ills besetting the Latin American economy are not determined by circumstantial or transient factors. They are an expression of the critical state of affairs in our time and of the incapacity of the economic system—owing to structural defects that it has been beyond our ability or our power to remedy—to achieve and maintain a rate of development consonant with the growth of the population and with its demands for a speedy improvement in its levels of living."[5]

The immensity of the overall task of economic and social changes facing all the Latin American peoples alike may be guaged from this authoritative opinion. Dr. Prebisch takes us back to the thesis advanced at the beginning of the present book when he insists:

> "The notion, which dies hard, that development takes place spontaneously, without a rational and deliberate effort to achieve it, has proved to be an illusion, both in Latin America and in the other peripheral regions of the world. For a century now our economies have been linked to the international economy, and fifty per cent of the population is still stagnating in pre-capitalist conditions which are incompatible with its growing economic and social aspirations."

Nevertheless, the passing examples which have already been

---

[5] Quoted from statement by Raul Prebisch, Executive-Secretary of ECLA, *Towards a Dynamic Development Policy for Latin America,* United Nations, New York, 1964.

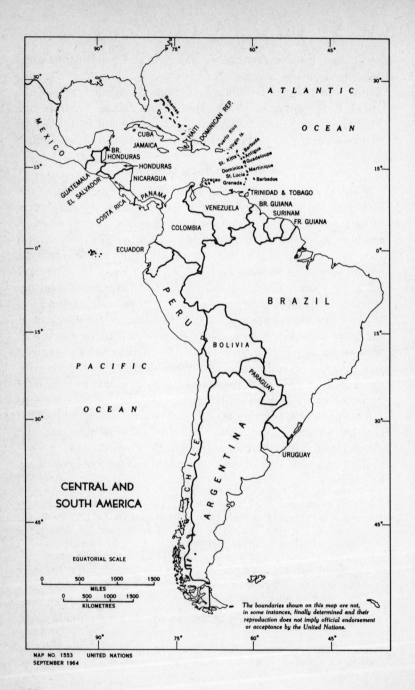

CENTRAL AND
SOUTH AMERICA

EQUATORIAL SCALE

MILES
0   500   1000   1500

KILOMETRES
0   500   1000   1500

The boundaries shown on this map are not,
in some instances, finally determined and their
reproduction does not imply official endorsement
or acceptance by the United Nations.

MAP NO. 1553   UNITED NATIONS
SEPTEMBER 1964

128

given of inroads already made by the UN and its agencies into this chronic backlog of poverty in Latin America, where other methods have patently failed, is an enheartening token of better things to come.

There is space to mention only one further phase of economic development in this huge sub-continent, and this concerns what has become known as "Central American Integration." The economic integration of Central America was first considered by ECLA in 1951 when, in compliance with the wishes of the governments of Costa Rica, El Salvador, Guatemala, Honduras, and Nicaragua, it established a Co-operation Committee among the countries concerned. The secretariat prepared studies on the ways and means of achieving that integration. Subsequently the Central American Economic Co-operation Committee was established on a permanent basis and Panama was invited to join as an observer. The Committee's task is to advise the governments on the gradual integration of the economies of the Central American isthmus. It encourages the co-ordination of the national programmes of economic development and co-ordinates technical assistance services under the programmes. The Committee receives regular support, of course, from the United Nations technical assistance programme and the Specialized Agencies.

A GIANT LINK

Economic integration in Central America is obviously a way out of the limitations imposed by the smallness of the five national markets. It will permit the establishment of types of industries requiring a market larger than that of any of the countries individually. Moreover, the unification of the five markets will lead progressively to over-all schemes of development in which the existing natural resources, manpower, and capital are put to the best possible use. To facilitate the fulfilment of these objectives, it has been necessary to study, from a regional standpoint, the possibilities of widening the basic economic services, such as transport, communications and electric power, and to carry out investigations of natural resources, manpower, trade, industrialization and agricultural development on a Central American scale.

Transport and communications are plainly part of these basic services and are vital for the growth of both agriculture and in-

Some seven million Indians live in the Andean highlands of Bolivia, Ecuador and Peru; mostly farmers, they eke out their lives at a bare subsistence level, struggling against a hostile nature. Today, five international organizations—United Nations, UNESCO, WHO, FAO and ILO—are working closely with the three governments in carrying out the Andean Indian programme.

dustry. At the request of the six Central American republics, the Special Fund and the World Bank have carried out a comprehensive survey of the telecommunications requirements of each of these countries and proposed a programme for the expansion of national networks and their linking to each other and to the rest of the world.

The report was submitted in March 1964, and recommends the construction of a 2,000-kilometre trunk line. This system would connect the capital cities of Costa Rica, El Salvador, Guatemala, Honduras, Nicaragua, and Panama by a 300-channel radio link running parallel to the Pan-American highway. At its northern end, it would tie in to a new radio link between Guatemala and Mexico, which in turn feeds into a radio link with the United

States; at its southern end, it would take advantage of an existing link in Panama between David and Panama City to reach the cable stretching under the Caribbean to Miami and Kingston, Jamaica. Thirty-one of the thirty-three transmitting stations along the single-route trunk would use the facilities of the national networks, which would be modernized to serve regional as well as national needs.

The consultants have estimated that the 300-channel link would cost some $6 million. It could be established in two years and would meet the region's needs until 1975. Approximately 70 per cent of the channels would be used for telephone and telegraph communications and 30 per cent for broadcasting. A television link could be added later. The report specifies equipment and personnel required for the regional linking of the national networks. Detailed proposals for the modernization of the domestic networks have also been prepared for each of the Governments and a number of them have begun implementation of the recommendations. Costa Rica has obtained a World Bank loan of $8.5 million towards the estimated cost of $12 million, and Ed Salvador has received a $9.5 million loan from the same source to help finance its $17 million telecommunications programme.

Thus, another giant link is being forged between the past and the future.

9

Looking To The Future

A fair sample of the pragmatic way in which the leaders of the developing world are looking to the future of their nations can be seen in a short speech which Julius K. Nyerere, President of Tanganyika and Zanzibar, delivered to the General Assembly of his country, announcing a five year development plan.*

He outlined a plan calling for an expenditure of 688 million dollars during the five-year period. This plan is the first of three, which will cover a period up to 1980. Its main objectives are to raise the annual *per capita* income in the United Republic of Tanganyika and Zanzibar from about $54 to $126, so as to make the country self-sufficient in trained manpower, and to raise life expectancy to 50 years from the present level of 35 to 40. Dr. Nyerere said that the country intended to spend about $140 million a year over the next five years. For this purpose, $324 million must be found from foreign private investment, if the plan is to succeed. "Private investors can provide this money," the President pointed out, "but they will only do so if they believe they can make a profit and be allowed to export that profit if they wish to do so. These conditions we must accept."

The President also urged that a common market was in the best interests of all East Africa. "I am pleased to report," he said, "that our brothers in Kenya and Uganda understand our problem and with their co-operation a solution has been found. In the future, a system of industrial licensing and import quotas between our three countries will enable each to share the benefits

---

* The United Republic is now named Tanzania.

132

of a common market." Stressing the immediate need for skilled workers, Dr. Nyerere said that the Government would have to recruit at least 500 people with high-level skills from abroad. In addition, the country needed 1,200 teachers to fulfill current educational objectives.[1]

In this skeleton prospectus of one new nation's needs, the reader can perceive the basic ingredients of the immense development task as it is presenting itself to country after country, namely: overall economic planning, raising *per capita* income within a brief period, increasing life expectancy, inviting foreign private investments, negotiating regional marketing, training manpower, and above all, EDUCATION. In the years ahead, all these separate but related claims from the developing countries will play an increasing role in the shaping of the United Nations system; for, unless the United Nations can respond fully to the needs of the majority of the peoples which compose it, its own future will be in doubt.

THE GLOBAL CHALLENGE

It is the purpose of this concluding chapter, therefore, to attempt to pull together the main threads of the response which the United Nations family is attempting to make to the divergent needs of the developing world where—it often seems—everything is everywhere wanted all at once. There is no precedent in history for this global appeal for outside "assistance" on so many levels and by so many people. The United Nations and its agencies have hardly had time to formulate a common policy or—excepting the older agencies—even build their organizations to cope with more than a fraction of the demands now being made upon them.

Says Professor Jan Tinbergen, Director of the Netherlands Economic Institute: "The world, characterized by a vast gap between technical ability and moral power, is in desperate need of a policy—a policy that gives it shape, and creates a framework for the solution of its urgent problems."[2] The earlier chapters have tried to show how that new framework has evolved almost

---

[1] *New York Times* (13 May 1964).
[2] Jan Tinbergen: *Shaping the World Economy*, 20th Century Fund, New York, 1962.

piecemeal in response to the pleas of the developing countries; but it has not been the purpose of this book to describe the political machinery by which a deliberate United Nations policy in these fields is or could be formulated. It is a fact, nonetheless, that the United Nations organization is the only entity, by its very existence, which has attempted to confront this global challenge with a global response.

At least, it is evident from the nature of the problems covered in the foregoing chapters, that the traditional procedures of unilateral "foreign aid" are demonstrably inadequate—if not obsolete. If, at this early stage, only the dim outlines of a co-ordinated United Nations policy or methodology can be seen, it is because the urgency of the tasks to be performed calls for action, rather than contemplation—for a programme, rather than a philosophy. Much of the UN's activity in development must be experimental; it must be flexible and pragmatic. A "policy", in the sense of a coherent list of politically acceptable principles, can only come *out* of the Development Decade—as is in fact happening—not precede it.[3]

In the final analysis, the United Nations will be judged by its decisions on specific programmes, rather than on its discussions on general issues. Nevertheless, since "co-ordination" of policy, a well as of programmes, has been a recurring theme both within the United Nations bodies and between the United Nations agencies—especially relating to the topics within the purview of the Economic and Social Council—a summary might here be attempted of some of the headings under which this co-ordination is in fact proceeding, with a view to future action and, maybe, the emergence of an eventual "policy".

THE MERGER PLAN

To begin with, the Secretary General proposed, for the acceptance of the General Assembly, that the two main programmes be merged into a "United Nations Development Programme." Under this plan, two existing operations aiding developing countries, the Expanded Programme of Technical Assistance and the

---

[3] See, for example, John G. Hadwen and Johan Kaufmann: *How United Nations Decisions Are Made.* Sythoff Publications, Leyden, 1963.

Special Fund, would be amalgamated. These merger proposals came before the United Nations Economic and Social Council meeting in Geneva in July 1964, whose recommendations go before the General Assembly later in the year.*

This act of consolidation will go a long way to streamline the activities of the Expanded Programme and the Special Fund, as well as to simplify organizational arrangements and facilitate over-all planning. The concern of all the aforementioned Committee's members was "so to organize the operations of the United Nations family in the economic and social field that it will be well-prepared and in a position to meet its growing responsibilities for assisting the developing nations."

It might be noted at this point that the 1964 United Nations Trade Conference in Geneva (see Chapter 7) asked the Special Fund to consider enlarging its activities to include investment proper. This proposal would have the Special Fund extend its program to include increased financing of demonstration projects and the undertaking of investment proper, as additional resources become available. The Special Fund would, in that event, be authorized to accept additional contributions for this purpose; but it would ensure that new responsibilities did not prejudice its pre-investment work.

That Conference also adopted a recommendation seeking to bring the proposed United Nations *Capital Development Fund* into operation at an early date. If eventually implemented, the Geneva resolution would have the Capital Development Fund start its operations soon in order to help finance development, especially in those countries at an earlier stage of development, as well as to advance national and regional plans in the field of industrialization. The resources of such a Capital Development Fund would be derived from voluntary contributions. It should be noted, however, that some of the countries which did

---

* In August 1964, the 37th session of ECOSOC recommended the UN General Assembly to combine the Expanded Programme of Technical Assistance and the Special Fund in a single programme to be known as the United Nations Development Programme (UNDP), on the understanding that the special functions of the two programmes, as well as two separate funds, should be maintained and contributions pledged separately as hitherto.

In a low-income housing area somewhere in Peru, a housewife answers questions by a census-taker, while curious children and neighbours look on; for a thorough campaign to arrive at a precise figure of population is an essential basis of social progress.

not vote for the proposal declared that, although they had often expressed sympathy for the idea of a United Nations Capital Development Fund, it was useless to press for it as long as the largest potential contributors were unreceptive to it. These latter countries favoured the alternative of strengthening and improving the Special Fund.[4]

READING, WRITING AND ARITHMETIC

In an entirely different field, looking to the future, the 1963 General Assembly had called for special action to support national efforts for the eradication of illiteracy. The view of UNESCO was that "strong motivations exist for a world-wide effort in favour of adult literacy," but that the world-wide literacy

[4] See also *Appendix 2* for excerpts from the 1964 Trade Conference "Final Act."

136

campaign should be regarded from now on, not as an end in itself, but as part of overall development, and so linked closely to technical and vocational training. UNESCO has accordingly outlined a plan of action calling for an experimental phase, with three years of intensive action in a few countries; followed by a period of evaluation; and later an attack on a world basis. An estimated $33 million would be needed for the initial phase. Already a start has been made to reduce to less shameful proportions the estimated figure of 700 million illiterate adults.

At the same time, the newly-established United Nations Advisory Committee on the Application of Science and Technology to Development has called for an immediate world-wide attack on a number of important scientific problems. Science and technology, the Committee believes, offer the promise of new and better ways of achieving economic development. But achieving such development requires great human and material investment. Small investments in research and development may, however, sometimes yield solutions which will greatly increase the return from large capital investments. One specific example of international co-operation to this end would be control of the tsetse fly, a problem on which action could be initiated quickly and inexpensively.

Modern science is not a magic wand, however, to be waved over a poor country to convert it into a rich one. The 1963 Conference made clear that the advance of scientific technology can only be regarded as one part of a concerted national programme of educational, economic, industrial, and social change. "A great deal of very detailed decision-making in the scientific and technical field", Professor P. N. S. Blackett of Britain told the Conference, "will fall on the Governments of the newly emerging countries, just at the time when vital political, economic and social problems have to be solved. So it is evident that a high priority for the educational system of an emerging country is the training of an adequate number of scientifically and technologically-minded executives able to make these complex and difficult decisions."[5]

5 *World of Opportunity*, (Vol. I of *Conference on Science and Technology* series) United Nations, New York, 1963.

Education—technical as well as general—has therefore become a top priority of the Development Decade. The aforementioned Committee began its work at United Nations Headquarters in February 1964. Through it world scientists are pooling their leadership in a concerted attack on specific problems of technical education, as well as on questions ranging from food supplies and health to industrialization in the developing areas. In the report of its first session, the 18-member Committee proposed such steps as the following:

(a) Creation of what might be regarded as an International Science Corps, through which scientists of the developed countries could contribute to world development;

(b) Supply of modern equipment for training and research to developing areas and the devising of new education and training systems appropriate to these areas;

(c) Establishment of more national and regional research centres, with staff trained to seek out the latest scientific information for local application;

(d) Designation of one central co-ordinating agency in each developing country to deal with all technical assistance available from the United Nations, its agencies, and other sources.

This expanding programme of scientific interest, which has become the concern of the whole UN family at this time, was well summed up in the message of U Thant to the Congress of Scientists on Survival, held in New York in June 1964:

"The task of serving as a clearing house of technical knowledge and experience on an international scale is one which is by no means new to the United Nations. In August of this year we will be inaugurating in Geneva the Third Conference on the Peaceful Uses of Atomic Energy. These Conferences have contributed to a new spirit of scientific objectivity and positive co-operation in the field of atomic energy. It was wisely remarked some years ago that 'To think of atomic energy in terms of the atom bomb is like thinking of electricity in terms of the electric chair.'

"A new area of scientific co-operation through the United

Nations is also developing in respect of the exciting exploration of outer space. Joint programmes are being devised so that as many nations as possible may share in the technical aspects of this work. I hope scientists will be encouraged by these developments to begin contemplating the possibility, not only of major international space projects, but also of joint research and development programmes on an international basis in other fields—for example, aeronautics, health, power generation and conversion, food production, as well as in the social sciences. Major commitments to such co-operative international ventures may be expected to create the confidence, mutual interest and trust that are a precondition for progress towards general disarmament."

STARTING NEW INDUSTRIES

Since so much of economic advance in the "new" countries will depend on the building of their industries, as we have seen, the need for technically trained people will be more than apparent. A number of promising industries in the underdeveloped areas already owe their existence, in part, to the United Nations. "A penicillin plant near Bombay provides one example," states Paul G. Hoffman: "In the beginning, the project was plagued by a multitude of troubles. The workers did not know what to do or how to do it. Some routines normally expected of a factory worker in an industrially advanced nation were incomprehensible to the men engaged to operate the penicillin plant. One by one the problems were licked. When it became evident that the plant was going to be successful, a number of other plants sprang up around it."[6]

In this connexion, the primary value of light industries for the developing countries should not be overlooked. "One school of thought" says the 1963 Geneva report, "is that a country without any significant industrial base should start by developing light industry, producing consumer goods. This would ease the problem of foreign currency by substituting imported goods with local manufacturers. Light industries require fewer resources and their capital turnover is more rapid; they are able to yield a quick profit and it is easier to train the labour force to man them; they

---

[6] Paul G. Hoffman: *World Without Want,* Harper and Row, New York, 1962.

can mean substantial savings in transport, serve local markets and create local employment."[7]

CUTTING OUT WASTE

On the reverse side of the medal of progress, there remains the intractable problem—raised in Chapter 2—of the universal reduction of armaments and, as a corollary, the conversion of war industries to peaceful uses. As we have noted, the Secretary-General and the heads of the various agencies have long had under consideration the specific problems involved in the utilization of savings from disarmament for aid to developing countries. One of the "principles" adopted by a big majority at the 1964 Trade and Development Conference in Geneva reads: "All countries recognize that a significant portion of resources released in successive stages as a result of the conclusion of an agreement on general and complete disarmament under effective international control should be allocated to the promotion of economic development in developing countries."

Since this gigantic effort will require extensive research and planning, both national and international, various plans to ensure the maintenance in the nations affected of such high levels of economic activity as will permit the diversion of resources to peaceful needs, are obviously necessary, or nothing will ever be done. For example, it is proposed that:

1. The Secretary-General should act as the central point of co-ordination in respect of all studies of the economic and social aspects of disarmament;
2. All members of the United Nations family undertaking such studies should prepare concerted programmes of work;
3. A committee representing the Specialized Agencies should be set up to co-operate with the Secretary-General in developing such a joint programme.

The possibility of joint action by the various member organizations of the United Nations family will naturally depend in large measure on the response made by Member States and on the

---

[7] *Industry* (Vol. IV of *Science and Technology for Development* series) United Nations, New York, 1963.

sincerity of their governments in carrying out their own plans directed towards the economic and social consequences of the general disarmament to which they have all *pledged* themselves in the General Assembly resolution. The Secretary-General has suggested that one important step would be for the States principally involved to set up for themselves what has been described as "an *economic* early-warning system to enable the authorities responsible for economic and social policy to take appropriate action to deal with the consequences of important cuts in defense spending."[8]

A NEW TRAINING AND RESEARCH INSTITUTE

In December 1963, the General Assembly asked the Secretary-General to take steps to set up a United Nations Training and Research Institute and to explore possible sources, both governmental and private, of financial assistance to it. Through its training and research activities, the proposed Institute "could make a unique contribution toward achieving the targets of the United Nations Development Decade and to enhancing the effectiveness of the United Nations itself." As one of its main tasks, the Institute would seek to build up a corps of trained personnel, particularly from the developing countries, for service with member governments and with organizations in the United Nations system.

In its other major field—research—the Institute could help to meet a need which has been often described as increasingly urgent and important. It might, for example, seek the most effective techniques for meeting Development Decades targets, analyze United Nations peacekeeping operations and suggest guidelines for the future, compare techniques for the pacific settlement of disputes, examine the economic and social implications of disarmament, consider questions involved in the field of human rights, and investigate ways of ensuring maximum benefits from science and technology.

But the proposed Institute can be brought into existence only if the necessary funds are obtained. Initial resources of $10 million, to cover five or six years of work, are envisaged, with firm pledges of not less than $5 million, which are desired before

---

[8] See *Economic and Social Consequences of Disarmament*, United Nations, New York, 1963.

operations can begin. A personal representative of the Secretary-General began a visit to a number of world capitals and major cities in the Spring of 1964 to seek financial support of this order and pledges are coming in.**

RUNNING HARD TO STAND STILL

Since we know today that, although half of the world population does not have enough to eat, the number of mouths to feed is growing at a truly explosive rate, the United Nations is compelled to handle both of these issues together. If population increases at nearly the same per cent as output of food, the net benefit per person is nil. Thus, it has been aptly said that many countries are having to run hard just to stand still.

On the positive side of this dilemma, the World Food Programme, which was established by the United Nations and FAO for an experimental period of three years, from 1st January 1963, has begun to contribute to the Development Decade in this emergency area. The combined exercise seeks as its major aim to stimulate economic and social development through aid in the form of food. Under it, food is used to supplement cash salaries paid to workers engaged in development projects, or food supplies may be provided to families resettled so as to tide them over pending the first harvest on their new land. The Programme has also been meeting urgent food needs. By the end of the first year of operations, 28 projects in 22 countries of Africa, the Americas, Asia, Europe and the Middle East had been approved. Among the projects already approved can be instanced Bolivia (land settlement in four areas), Chad, Africa (land reclamation and school feeding), Pakistan (post-cyclone reconstruction), Syria (development of nomadic sheep husbandry), Turkey (establishment of

---

** The United Nations began in 1961 a systematic analysis of the inter-relationship of social and economic development, and the Government of the Netherlands made available to the United Nations one million dollars to establish a research institute for this purpose. The Institute opened in Geneva on 1 July 1964, with the appointment of a Director and nucleus staff. Its Governing Board includes eminent social scientists and the heads of the regional development planning Institutes in Asia, Africa and Latin America. The programme of the Institute aims essentially to bring out the contribution of the *human factors* involved in economic progress and development.

142

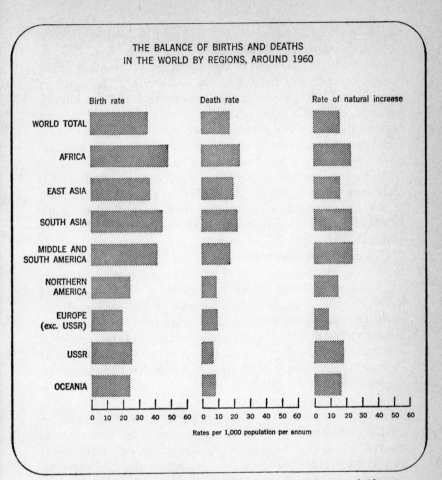

THE BALANCE OF BIRTHS AND DEATHS
IN THE WORLD BY REGIONS, AROUND 1960

Birth rate   Death rate   Rate of natural increase

WORLD TOTAL

AFRICA

EAST ASIA

SOUTH ASIA

MIDDLE AND
SOUTH AMERICA

NORTHERN
AMERICA

EUROPE
(exc. USSR)

USSR

OCEANIA

0 10 20 30 40 50 60   0 10 20 30 40 50 60   0 10 20 30 40 50 60

Rates per 1,000 population per annum

nine model villages), and Yugoslavia (reconstruction of Skopje after the earthquake); and many more will follow. The resources of the Programme come from voluntary contributions pledged by more than 60 members of the United Nations and of FAO, including a number of developing countries themselves.

On what might be considered the negative side, the study of population trends has become and will become of increasing concern to the UN, since it lies conspicuously across the route of the Decade. The first World Population Conference was held in Rome in 1954, under UN auspices. It did much to improve inter-

143

national understanding of population problems and to promote scientific research into these problems.

Since that time, the rates of population growth in many of the developing countries have gone on accelerating. The censuses taken around 1960 have helped to further research into population problems, especially in the developing countries. For such reasons as these, the General Assembly recommended that a second World Population Conference should be convened, and that arrangements be made for the fullest participation of representatives from the less-developed countries. This Conference will accordingly be held in Belgrade, Yugoslavia, in the autumn of 1965. It will be a scientific meeting of experts from all parts of the World, and its aims will be especially related to problems of economic and social development.[9]

The recent multiplication of population poses difficult problems for the developing countries, confronted as they are with its implications for the success of their efforts to raise the levels of living. The problem is further complicated by the swelling stream of migrants who are pouring into the cities from the countryside. Yet present knowledge of population trends and of their economic and social consequences is not sufficient to provide a sound basis for national decisions in most cases. If present trends continue, an even higher rate of increase would soon be *typical* of less-developed regions.

Some Governments have already decided to take measures for the purpose of modifying these trends, but other Governments are still considering the need for similar action and what form it should take. That there exist less pessimistic points-of-view became evident, for example, at the 1963 scientific gatherings in Geneva, when Father Clement Mertens of the Holy See declared: "We have frequently spoken of over-population and very seldom of under-population. And yet there is no doubt that economic development in certain regions, in particular in Latin America and in Central and South America, is hampered by insufficient population density. Therefore, if we wish to facilitate economic progress in these regions, we must hope that they will have a

[9] See *World Population Conference 1965*, Information Bulletin No. 1, United Nations, New York, 1964.

144

sufficiently high population and birth rate and we must assist them in fulfilling this need in an appropriate fashion."[10]

PROMISE OF THE FUTURE

Finally, the promise of the future has already become symbolised, if not as yet actualised, in the designation of the twentieth year of the United Nations as International Co-operation Year. On November 21, 1963, the governments of the world, acting through the U.N. General Assembly, called on private organizations and individuals everywhere to join the whole United Nations family in a worldwide effort in 1965 to intensify international co-operation on a scale never before attempted.

The original suggestion for International Co-operation Year came from the late Prime Minister Nehru in a speech before the 1961 General Assembly, when he said:

> "The essential thing about this world is co-operation, and even today, between countries which are opposed to each other in the political or other fields, there is a vast amount of co-operation. Little is known, or little is said, about this co-operation that is going on but a great deal is said about every point of conflict, and so the world is full of this idea that the conflicts go on, and we live on the verge of disaster. Perhaps it would be a truer picture if the co-operating elements in the world today were put forward and we were made to think that the world depends on co-operation and not on conflict."

The Resolution designating 1965 International Co-operation Year called on the various "branches" of the United Nations and the Non-Governmental Organizations to publicize to the widest extent possible the activities of international co-operation in which they were already engaged, as well as to expand those activities. They were asked to formulate the programmes as seemed to them appropriate, and to report to a 12-member Committee on International Co-operation, which has already been working on suggestions submitted through private international organizations, as well as Governments. The Committee approved the design for a

10 *People and Living* (Vol. V of *Science and Technology for Development* series), United Nations, New York, 1963.

United Nations postage stamp, bearing a symbol of ICY, two hands clasped over a laurel wreath. This stylized design is being sent to all Member Governments suggesting that they produce an ICY stamp of the same design in their own currency.

Universities and other institutions of higher learning are being urged to schedule courses on International Co-operation, in which the possibilities of extending such co-operation can be systematically explored. Universities are also asked to review their teaching on the United Nations and to bring it up-to-date. Governments have been prompted to ratify existing international agreements during 1965, such as the Conventions on Law of the Sea, on Human Rights and on increasing the free flow of Educational Scientific and Cultural Materials between countries. Governments, too, and voluntary organizations have been urged to standardize symbols which would aid in international understanding, such as road signs, danger signals at sea and so forth, which vary in different parts of the world.

"The primary task of the U.N. Committee," stated ambassador Ralph Enckell of Finland, Chairman of the Committee, "is first and foremost to arouse interest in the Year of International Co-operation, to provoke, to inspire and to stimulate suitable activities and initiatives. Our role is to a great extent to co-ordinate the efforts of governments, specialized agencies and non-governmental organizations. Our main contribution is to see to it that appropriate publicity be given to international co-operation in 1965 and to highlight important manifestations. Most efforts have to be made by individual Member-States and each State will certainly know best what it should do and how it should embark upon such a task in order best to achieve the desired results."

IT IS NOT ENOUGH

Thus, the United Nations family of organizations looks beyond its immediate programme and plans ahead. There can be no respite in the foreseeable future—nor is any sought by the world citizens who staff its operations or serve its institutions.

Only a glimpse of their manifold activities in the economic and social field has been possible in the foregoing pages. But the Development Decade will succeed or will fail not solely because of them, but in the degree that "We, the Peoples" sustain them

"Our Decade of Development cannot ultimately succeed unless it is rooted in the wills and hearts of millions of citizens everywhere"
—U Thant.

or ignore them in their labours. As U Thant said, in addressing a student audience at Copenhagen, in May 1962:

"It is not enough for us in the United Nations to dedicate ourselves to the Decade of Development. We have to take with us the governments to whom we are responsible and through them we have to reach out to the peoples. . . . Our Decade of Development cannot ultimately succeed unless it is rooted in the wills and hearts of millions of citizens everywhere. It will not succeed unless it can win their sustained support. It will not succeed unless they see it as a great goal of human endeavour and one which they are prepared to make their own."

Further Reading

(a) General Books

Asher, Robert E.: *The United Nations and Promotion of the General Welfare*, The Brookings Institution, Washington, D.C., 1957.

Black, Eugene R.: *The Diplomacy of Economic Development*, Cambridge, Harvard University Press, 1960.

Clark, Colin: *The Conditions of Economic Progress*, London, Macmillan; New York, St. Martin's Press, 1957.

Hicks, John R.: *Essays in World Economics*, Oxford, Clarendon Press, 1959.

Higgins, Benjamin: *Economic Development: Principles, Problems and Policies*, Norton, New York, 1959.

Hirschman, Albert O.: *The Strategy of Economic Development*, Yale University Press, New Haven, 1958; Oxford University Press, London, 1959.

Hoffman, Paul G.: *World Without Want*, Harper and Row, New York, 1963.

Joyce, J. Avery: *Challenge of the Decade of Development*, Coward-McCann, New York, 1965.

The Story of International Co-operation, Watts, New York, 1964.

Lewis, W. Arthur: *The Theory of Economic Growth*, George Allen & Unwin Ltd., London, 1955.

Myrdal, Gunnar: *Economic Theory and Under-Developed Regions*, Duckworth, London, 1955.

Challenge to Affluence, Pantheon, New York, 1963.

Nurkse, Ragnar: *Problems of Capital Formation in Underdeveloped Countries*, Blackwell, Oxford, 1962.

Pearson, Lester & Others: *Restless Nations*, Dodd, Mead & Co., New York, 1962.

Rostow, W.W.: *The Stages of Economic Growth*, Cambridge University Press, 1960.

Shonfield, Andrew: *The Attack on World Poverty*, Vintage, New York, 1962.

Singer, Hans: *International Development: Growth and Change*, intro. by Paul Hoffman, McGraw-Hill, New York, 1964.

Staley, Eugene: *The Future of Underdeveloped Countries: Political Implications of Economic Development*, Harper, New York, 1961.

Tinbergen, Jan: *Shaping the World Economy*, 20th Century Fund, New York, 1962.

Ward, Barbara: *The Rich and the Poor Nations*, Norton, New York, 1962.

Wood, J. Duncan: *Building the Institutions of Peace*, Allen & Unwin, London, 1962.

(b) *United Nations Publications*

(These publications may be purchased from the nearest bookseller who stocks United Nations books. If in doubt as to his address, write to the Sales Section in New York.)

A Handbook of Public Administration, (126 pp). Current practice with special reference to developing countries.

The United Nations Development Decade: Proposals for Action, English, French and Spanish. Some of the subjects covered are: mobilization of human resources, capital assistance, international trade, development of natural resources, transport and communications, housing and urban development, and other social problems of the developing countries.

Adventure in Development, English (29 pp). A booklet describing the technical aid programmes offered by the United Nations and its related agencies for the low-income countries.

Aspects of Economic Development, English (84 pp)· An illustrated booklet presenting in outline some of the main aspects of the economic development process; including the production of more food, the improvement of health, the spread of education, and promotion of social welfare.

Impact: A UN Special Fund Report. English (36 pp)· Illustrated report describing the Special Fund's current programme.

A Study of Industrial Growth, English, French and Spanish (55 p). A study to determine the level and structure of industrialization of individual countries in the light of their needs, resources and policies.

Processes and Problems of Industrialization in Under-developed Countries, English and Spanish (152 pp). The industrialization process in a number of countries in the early stages of economic development and means of assisting under-developed countries to industrialize rapidly.

Establishment of Industrial Estates in Under-developed Countries, English, French and Spanish (58 pp). A discussion of objectives and policies followed in establishing industrial estates in developed and under-developed countries.

The Capital Development Needs of the Less-Developed Countries, English, French and Spanish (53 pp).

Economic Development, Planning and International Co-operation, English and Spanish (65 pp). A study of the Latin American countries' need to reform the economic and social structure.

Measures for the Economic Development of Under-Developed Countries, English, French and Spanish (108 pp).

United Nations Conference on Trade and Development: A Search for Practical Action. Summarizes problems facing the Conference, suggested solutions, the chronological background and reference sources.

Towards a New Trade Policy for Development. 125-page report of the Secretary-General of the Conference, Dr. Raul Prebisch.

The Expanded Programme of Technical Assistance. English, French and Spanish (20 pp). An illustrated booklet giving concrete meaning to the Decade.

Economic Survey of Africa Since 1950, United Nations, New York, 1959.

Economic Survey of Asia and the Far East, United Nations, Bangkok. (Published annually).

Economic Survey of Latin America, United Nations, Santiago. (Published annually).

World Economic Survey, United Nations, New York. (Published annually).

SCIENCE AND TECHNOLOGY FOR DEVELOPMENT. These volumes are derived from the United Nations Conference on the Application of Science and Technology for the Benefit of the Less-Developed Areas, Geneva, 1963:

Volume One: *World of Opportunity,* a summary and review of the Conference and analysis of its achievements.

Volume Two: *Natural Resources,* planning and policy for the development of land, water, minerals and energy.

Volume Three: *Agriculture,* problems faced by developing nations and some of the solutions evolved in more advanced ones.

Volume Four: *Industry,* a discussion of the need for planning, priorities, and location and manpower problems.

Volume Five: *People and Living,* a study of population, health, nutrition, rural development and urbanization.

Volume Six: *Education and Training,* a general survey and a study of major factors in national education programmes.

Volume Seven: *Science and Planning,* the strategy and techniques of planning and various devices for implementation.

Volume Eight: *Plenary Proceedings,* reference volume to the Conference, including the list of papers and index.

UN-UNESCO Study Guide Series, Oceana Publications, N. Y., 1962-4:

This series of study-guides brings together detailed information presented in a broad historical context, on the structure and work of the United Nations and its related agencies.

Vol. 1.   "World Pace and the United Nations" (peace-keeping organs, International Court of Justice, refugees).

Vol. 2.   "Food for Life—Food for Thought" (FAO and UNESCO).

Vol. 3.   "Improving Living Conditions" (WHO and ILO).

Vol. 4.   "Pooling Skills for Human Progress" (technical assistance and atomic energy).

Vol. 5.   "World Peace and Human Dignity" (UN purposes, human rights).

Vol. 6.   "World of Promise" by J. Avery Joyce (Development Decade, World Trade, World Bank, Special Fund, and Technical Assistance programs).

(c) *UNESCO Publications*
(reprints)

(UNESCO publications may be ordered from the nearest book-seller, or direct from the National Distributor of UNESCO publications. They are available, in the United States from the National Distributors: UNESCO Publications Center, 317 East 34th Street, New York 10016, N. Y., or Columbia University Press, 2960 Broadway, New York 10027, N. Y. They are also on sale at the United Nations Bookshop, United Nations Building, New York.)

The Community Factor in Modern Technology (1960)
Education in a Technological Society (1959)
International Co-operation and Programmes of Economic and Social Development (1961)
International Migration and Economic Development (1961)
Measuring the Results of Development Projects (1961)
Social Aspects of Economic Development in Latin America (1963)
Social Change and Economic Development (1963)

(d) *Free Publications on World Bank*

(Requests for free publications on the World Bank should be addressed to the Office at 1818 H Street, N.W., Washington 25, D.C., or 4 Avenue d'Iéna, Paris 16s, France.)

Annual Report: The Bank, IFC and IDA.—each agency publishes an annual report. Issued in September. (English, French, German and Spanish.)
World Bank and IDA: Folding leaflet. (English, French, German, Italian and Spanish.)
The Activities of the World Bank and its Affiliates, by George D. Woods, text of an address before United Nations Economic and Social Council, 1963.
World Bank Loans at Work: Pictures, maps and text. (30-page illustrated booklet.)
The Growing World: Economic Development and the World Bank, by Robert L. Heilbroner. (*Public Affairs Pamphlet* No. 237.)

Appendix 1

on the

UNITED NATIONS DEVELOPMENT DECADE

The General Assembly,
Bearing in mind the solemn undertaking embodied in the Charter of the United Nations to promote social progress and better standards of life in larger freedom and to employ international machinery for the advancement of the economic and social development of all peoples,

Considering that the economic and social development of the economically less developed countries is not only of primary importance to those countries but is also basic to the attainment of international peace and security and to a faster and mutually beneficial increase in world prosperity . . .

1. *Designates* the current decade as the "United Nations Development Decade", in which Member States and their peoples will intensify their efforts to mobilize and to sustain support for the measures required on the part of both developed and developing countries to accelerate progress towards self-sustaining growth of the economy of the individual nations and their social advancement so as to attain in each under-developed country a substantial increase in the rate of growth, with each country setting its own target, taking as the objective a minimum annual rate of growth of aggregate national income of 5 per cent at the end of the Decade;

2. *Calls upon* States Members of the United Nations or members of the specialized agencies:

(*a*) To pursue policies designed to enable the less developed countries and those dependent on the export of a small range of primary commodities to sell more of their products at stable and remunerative prices in expanding markets, and thus to finance increasingly their own economic development from their earnings of foreign exchange and domestic savings;

(*b*) To pursue policies designed to ensure to the developing countries an equitable share of earnings from the extraction and marketing of their natural resources by foreign capital, in accordance with the generally accepted reasonable earnings on invested capital;

(*c*) To pursue policies that will lead to an increase in the flow of de-

153

velopment resources, public and private, to developing countries on mutually acceptable terms;

(d) To adopt measures which will stimulate the flow of private investment capital for the economic development of the developing countries, on terms that are satisfactory both to the capital-exporting countries and the capital-importing countries;

3. *Requests* the Secretary-General to communicate to the Governments of Member States any documentation useful for the study and application of the present resolution and to invite them to make proposals, if possible, concerning the contents of a United Nations programme for the Decade and the application of such measures in their respective plans;

4. *Requests* the Secretary-General, taking account of the views of Governments and in consultation, as appropriate, with the heads of international agencies with responsibilities in the financial, economic and socal fields, the Managing Director of the Special Fund, the Executive Chairman of the Technical Assistance Board, and the regional economic commissions, to develop proposals for the intensification of action in the fields of economic and social development by the United Nations system of organizations, with particular reference, *inter alia,* to the following approaches and measures designed to further the objective of paragraph 1 above:

(a) The achievement and acceleration of sound self-sustaining economic development in the less developed countries through industralization, diversification and the development of a highly productive agricultural sector;

(b) Measures for assisting the developing countries, at their request, to establish well-conceived and integrated country plans—including, where appropriate, land reform—which will serve to mobilize internal resources and ot utilize resources offered by foreign sources on both a bilateral and a multilateral basis for progress towards self-sustained growth;

(c) Measures to improve the use of international institutions and instrumentalities for furthering economic and social development;

(d) Measures to accelerate the elimination of illiteracy, hunger and disease, which seriously affect the productivity of the people of the less developed countries;

(e) The need to adopt new measures, and to improve existing measures, for further promoting education in general and vocational and technical training in the developing countries with the co-operation, where appropriate, of the specialized agencies and States which can provide assistance in these fields, and for training competent national personnel in the fields of public administration, education, engineering, health and agronomy;

(f) The intensification of research and demonstration as well as other efforts to exploit scientific and technological potentialities of high promise for accelerating economic and social development;

(g) Ways and means of finding and furthering effective solutions in the field of trade in manufacturers as well as in primary commodities, bearing in mind, in particular, the need to increase the foreign exchange earnings of the under-developed countries;

(h) The need to review facilities for the collection, collation, analysis and dissemination of statistical and other information required for charting economic and social development and for providing constant measurement of progress towards the objectives of the Decade;

(*i*) The utilization of resources released by disarmament for the purpose of economic and social development, in particular of the under-developed countries;

(*j*) The ways in which the United Nations can stimulate and support realization of the objectives of the Decade through the combined efforts of national and international institutions, both public and private;

5. *Further requests* the Secretary-General to consult Member States, at their request, on the application of such measures in their respective development plans;

6. *Invites* the Economic and Social Council to accelerate its examination of, and decision on, principles of international economc co-operation directed towards the improvement of world economic relations and the stimulation of international co-operation;

7. *Requests* the Secretary-General to present his proposals for such a programme to the Economic and Social Council at its thirty-fourth session for its consideration and appropriate action;

8. *Invites* the Economic and Social Council to transmit the Secretary-General's recommendations, together with its views and its report on actions undertaken thereon, to States Members of the United Nations or members of the specialized agencies and to the General Assembly at its seventeenth session.

(*1084th plenary meeting, 19 December 1961.*)

Appendix 2

GENERAL PRINCIPLES

The Conference recommended the following General Principles to govern international trade relations and trade policies conducive to development:

I

Economic relations between countries, including trade relations, shall be based on respect for the principles of sovereign quality of states, self-determination of peoples, and non-interference in the internal affairs of other countries.

II

There shall be no discrimination on the basis of differences in socio-economic systems. Adaptation of trading methods shall be consistent with this principle.

III

Every country has the sovereign right freely to trade with other countries, and freely to dispose of its natural resources in the interest of the economic development and well-being of its own people.

IV

Economic development and social progress should be the common concern of the whole international community and should by increasing economic prosperity and well-being help strengthen peaceful relations and cooperation among nations. Accordingly, all countries pledge themselves to pursue internal and external economic policies designed to accelerate economic growth throughout the world, and in particular to help promote in developing countries a rate of growth consistent with the need to bring about substantial and steady increase in average income in order to narrow the gap between the standard of living in developing countries and that in the developed countries.

V

National and international economic policies should be directed towards the attainment of an international division of labour in harmony with the

157

needs and interests of developing countries in particular and of the world as a whole.

Developed countries should assist the developing countries in their efforts to speed up their economic and social progress, should cooperate in measures taken by developing countries for diversifying their economies and should encourage appropriate adjustments in their own economies to this end.

VI

International trade is one of the most important factors in economic development. It should be governed by such rules as are consistent with the attainment of economic and social progress and should not be hampered by measures incompatible therewith. All countries should cooperate in creating conditions of international trade conducive in particular to the achievement of a rapid increase in the export earnings of developing countries and in general to the promotion of an expansion and diversification of trade between all countries, whether at similar levels of development, at different levels of development, or having different economic and social systems.

VII

The expansion and diversification of international trade depends upon increasing access to markets, and upon remunerative prices for the exports of primary products. Developed countries shall progressively reduce and, in appropriate cases, eliminate barriers and other restrictions that hinder trade and consumption of products of particular interest to developing countries and take positive measures such as will create and increase markets for the exports of developing countries. All countries should cooperate though suitable international arrangements on an orderly basis in implementing measures designed to increase and stabilize primary commodity export earnings, particularly of developing countries, at equitable and remunerative prices and to maintain a mutually acceptable relationship between the prices of manufactured goods and those of primary products.

VIII

International trade should be conducted to mutual advantage on the basis of the most favoured nation treatment and should be free from measures detrimental to the trading interests of other countries. However, developed countries should grant concessions to all developing countries and extend to developing countries all concessions they grant to one another and should not, in granting these or other concessions, require any concessions in return from developing countries. New preferential concessions, both tariff and non-tariff, should be made to developing countries as a whole and such preferences should not be extended to developed countries. Developing countries need not extend to developed countries preferential treatment in operation amongst them. Special preferences at present enjoyed by certain developing countries in certain developed countries should be regarded as transitional and subject to progressive reduction· They should be eliminated as and when effective international measures guaranteeing at least equivalent advantages to the countries concerned come into operation.

IX

Developed countries participating in regional economic groupings should do their utmost to ensure that their economic integration does not cause injury to, or otherwise adversely affect, the expansion of their imports from third countries, and in particular from developing countries, either individually or collectively.

X

Regional economic groupings, integration or other forms of economic cooperation should be promoted among developing countries as a means of expanding their intra-regional and extra-regional trade and encouraging their economic growth and their industrial and agricultural diversification with due regard to the special features of development of the various countries concerned, as well as their economic and social systems. It will be necessary to ensure that such cooperation makes an effective contribution to the economic development of these countries, and does not inhibit the economic development of other developing countries outside such groupings.

XI

International institutions and developed countries should provide an increasing net flow of international financial, technical and economic assistance to support and reinforce, by supplementing the export earnings of developing countries, the efforts made by them to accelerate their economic growth through diversification, industrialization and increase of productivity on the basis of their national policies, plans and programmes of economic development. Such assistance should not be subject to any political or military conditions. This assistance, whatever its form and from whatever source, including foreign public and private loans and capital, should flow to developing countries on terms fully in keeping with their trade and development needs. International financial and monetary policies should be designed to take full account of the trade and development needs of developing countries.

XII

All countries recognize that a significant portion of resources released in successive stages as a result of the conclusion of an agreement on general and complete disarmament under effective international control should be allocated to the promotion of economic development in developing countries.

XIII

The Conference decided to include, as a separate part of the Principles adopted by the Conference, the Principles relating to transit trade of land-locked countries (referred to in this summary).

XIV

Complete decolonization in compliance with the United Nations Declaration on the Granting of Independence to Colonial Countries and Peoples and the liquidation of the remnants of colonialism in all its forms is a necessary condition for economic development and the exercise of sovereign rights over natural resources.

XV

The adoption of international policies and measures for the economic development of the developing countries shall take into account the individual characteristics and different stages of development of the developing countries, special attention being paid to the less developed among them, as an effective means of ensuring sustained growth with equitable opportunity for each developing country.

Appendix 3

List of Abbreviations

(USED IN THIS BOOK)

ACC	Administrative Committee on Co-ordination
ECA	Economic Commission for Africa
ECAFE	Economic Commission for Asia and the Far East
ECE	Economic Commission for Europe
ECLA	Economic Commission for Latin America
ECOSOC	Economic and Social Council
EPTA	Expanded Programme of Technical Assistance
FAO	Food and Agriculture Organization of the United Nations
IAEA	International Atomic Energy Agency
IBRD	International Bank for Reconstruction and Development
ICAO	International Civil Aviation Organization
IDA	International Development Association
IFC	International Finance Corporation
ILO	International Labour Organisation
IMF	International Monetary Fund
ITU	International Telecommunication Union
OAS	Organization of American States
OPEX	Programme for the provision of operational, executive and administrative personnel
OPI	Office of Public Information—United Nations Secretariat
TAB	Technical Assistance Board
TAC	Technical Assistance Committee
UNESCO	United Nations Educational, Scientific and Cultural Organization
UNICEF	United Nations Children's Fund
UNTA	United Nations Technical Assistance
WHO	World Health Organization
WMO	World Meteorological Organization

NOTE: All sums of money are expressed in United States dollars unless otherwise indicated. The charts and diagrams are in some cases based on provisional figures.

SUBJECT INDEX
(References to main topics)

STUDY GUIDE SERIES

*Also in separate booklets. Special quantity prices for schools and organizations on request.

Cloth volumes: 1-5, each	$ 2.50	Paper: Vol. 6,	$1.75
Set of 5 volumes:	$12.50	Set of 5 volumes:	$7.50
Special Vol. 6, cloth:	$ 3.50		